Property of
Curtis L. Freemont

Creative financing
avoiding the pitfalls

**Jeff Wride
Richard Ratliff**

Reston Publishing Co., Inc.
A Prentice-Hall Company
Reston, Virginia

Library of Congress Cataloging in Publication Data

Wride, Jeff.
  Creative financing.
  Includes index.
  1. Real property—Finance. 2. Real estate investment. 3. Mortgage loans. I. Ratliff, Richard C. II. Title.
HD1375.R33   1984   332.7'22   83-13660
ISBN 0-8359-1164-0   ISBN 0-8359-1162-4 (pbk.)

© 1984 by Reston Publishing Company, Inc.
A Prentice-Hall Company
Reston, Virginia 22090

All rights reserved. No part of this book may be reproduced, in any way or by any means, without permission in writing from the publisher.

10 9 8 7 6 5 4 3 2 1

Printed in the United States of America

Contents

Preface 1

1 **Investment goals** 2

This information can help investors develop their investment strategies.

2 **Introduction to creative financing** 10

Contains five real cases illustrating the consequences of properly and improperly utilizing creative-financing techniques. Sets the stage for later, more detailed chapters about those techniques and their dangers.

3 **Creative financing** 24

Describes creative, or owner, financing and how it differs from conventional financing methods. Includes some of the forms used in the creative-financing transaction.

4 Contract chains 36

Describes the dangers of contract chains—created when a property is sold from buyer to buyer, each retaining an obligation to continue paying over time—and how to avoid those dangers.

5 Balloon payments 46

Discusses how the purposes of balloon payments have been corrupted in the recent wave of owner-financed properties, and the dangers of balloon payments for both buyer and seller.

6 Negative cash flows 56

Not only the dangers of buying property with a negative cash flow, but the dangers of selling property with a negative cash flow for the new buyer. How to avoid cash flow problems.

7 No money down 68

Attacks this highly touted principle from the perspective of buyer and seller.

8 Borrowing for a downpayment 74

Shows how borrowing for a downpayment almost inevitably results in dangerously high negative cash flows. Presents an example used by a famous author arguing for the strategy of borrowing for a downpayment.

9 Subordinations and double closings 82

Discusses the problem of passing title of a property before receiving any compensation as downpayment. Contrasts the proper rise of this practice with its abuses.

10	**Handyman specials** 88	

How to predict the effectiveness of this investment strategy.

11	**"Due on sale" clauses** 92	

The value of "due on sale" clauses, and how many people avoid complying with their provisions—only to encounter problems later.

12	**Price vs. value** 96	

Demonstrates that a property really has only one value, despite the fact that creative financing methods often produce more than one price.

13	**Forfeiture and foreclosure** 106	

Forfeiture and foreclosure provisions, often appearing to be adequate protection for the seller against nonpayment by the buyer, may prove to be seriously deficient. How to avoid the problems.

14	**Qualifying the buyer** 114	

How to qualify the buyer yourself or to hire a professional to do it for you.

15	**Selling the tough property** 126	

Discusses how to sell these hard-to-sell properties in poor condition, in a bad location, or with poor design.

16	**The time value of money** 134	

What the hammer and saw are to the carpenter, an understanding of the time value of money is to the real estate investor.

17 Buying and selling real estate contracts 148

For those with enough cash, an attractive alternative to buying and selling real estate is buying and selling contracts. The returns might knock your socks off.

18 Taxes 154

Introduces some basic principles of taxation as they relate to real estate transactions.

19 Other important stuff 162

Miscellaneous issues which, considered together, can make a significant difference between a successful purchase/sale and an unsuccessful one.

20 The consummate real estate investor 172

Outlines the major problems and remedies associated with creative-financing techniques.

Glossary 180
Suggested reading 196
Index 198

Preface

Many books have been written about real estate investment using creative financing techniques, seemingly all about how to get rich at it. This book stresses that creative financing has disadvantages as well as advantages. We have seen no other book remotely like it. It is written for the novice investor and for the homeowner who may be considering selling. The book is short and easy to read. It is, however, solidly packed with information, including numerous short illustrations about the experiences of real people. Some of the information most likely will be new, and valuable even for the experienced investor. It is especially valuable for people selling property, since it is the only book we know addressing problems created for the seller by creative financing and how to avoid them.

    We hope that our readers will enjoy this book and that it will help them make better-informed decisions about how they use creative financing either in buying and selling family residences or in investment properties. We have had fun writing it. We hope you enjoy reading it.

Investment goals

Investors must determine their objectives before making any decisions about what properties to buy, how much to pay, or how to finance them. The naive investor might simply want to make money, that is, increase wealth. A goal such as this is not specific enough to guide decisions in real estate investment. Frequent goals that more experienced investors have for properties include the following:

- appreciation of property values
- cash inflow
- tax shelters
- use of the property as a dwelling, business investment, or some combination of family dwelling and investment

1

These goals can be broken down further into time frames—short-term vis-à-vis long-term. For example, one investor may want to invest in real estate as a hedge against future inflation. This investor's concern is not immediate cash flow from the property, but the increase of wealth as property values increase over future years. Another investor, however, may want to sell property soon after its purchase to make a short-term profit.

Both short-term and long-term goals can include all of the general goal categories outlined above. In a time of rapid inflation, property can appreciate in value significantly in a few weeks or months. Also, some investors "force" appreciation of property values. For example, a building in bad repair may be purchased at a bargain price and later refurbished, greatly increasing its value.

Appreciation of property values usually is associated

Follow the yellow brick road

with long-term goals. A frequent investment strategy is to purchase property with the intent of holding it for several years in the hopes that it will increase in value over that time.

One typical short-term goal is cash flows. Usually this goal is combined with a longer-term goal so that the short-term cash flows provide resources for expanded investments. The point is that there may be an objective to generate immediate cash flow. Some investments provide a regular, periodic cash flow, such as rental properties, or properties sold on contract. Other investments can provide an immediate cash flow, such as a sale where the buyer pays the total price at the time of sale. It is not unusual for investors to sell one piece of property simply to acquire short-term cash to invest in another property.

The income tax laws have created tax shelters allowing investors to purchase particular types of property that will delay sizeable tax liabilities for years. The short-term effect is to decrease current taxes. The long-term effect usually is to decrease the amount of taxes to be paid on the money invested in and earned from the property. Investors interested in tax shelters should consult with a qualified tax accountant or tax lawyer.

Investors also must determine how they want to use the property that they purchase. For the home-buyer the objective is simple. Other investors may want to live in a piece of property for a while and then sell it, simply hold it as an investment, or, if the building is a multi-unit residential property, the choice may be a combination of living quarters and investment.

Whatever the goal may be, the more specific it is the better. Notice that you must determine the nature of the goal you have and also some sort of time reference. We asked a successful investor what his goals were for the last piece of property he looked at. We did this simply to verify that successful investors do have very specific goals for the individual properties they purchase. He said that he had looked at a piece of property that day on which he had made an offer to buy. His goals for the property were to buy and resell quickly to a new buyer; he plans to raise the interest rate and then finance the loan himself for the new buyer, to make a profit and receive a regular cash flow over the next 30 years. It is important to note that this goal was specific to the property itself.

Further questioning revealed that this investor had formulated multiple goals—all specific—relating to all of his investments. Here is a sample listing:

"I plan to buy, on the average, one residential unit each month for the rest of my life. . . . I want to have bought 500 residential units by the time I am 50 years old." The investor defined a unit to be one residential housing unit. A duplex, for example, would have two units, a fourplex would have four units, and so forth.

"I want to earn $6,000 per month in net cash flow within five years."

Every investor should formulate various goals, some short-term and some long-term, all dealing with various aspects of the investor's business. Remember, the more specific they are, the better. Goals also should be flexible and reviewed from time-to-time for needed changes. There are numerous references that can lead you step-by-step through realistic and effective goal setting. In order to be successful you must begin with goals because every other investment decision must be coordinated with your goals.

Property selection

Numerous considerations determine whether a particular property is a desirable investment. Important ones are discussed below.

Compatibility with investment goals

The first consideration in the evaluation of any property is whether it helps accomplish your investment goals. If not, forget it.

Price

The price must be in acccordance with your resources and the true value of the property. If the price is beyond your resources or if the property is over-priced, then you may incur unnecessary risk of financial losses. Generally, price is determined by some kind of systematic appraisal.

Financing terms

These terms include the amount and timing of payments. They comprise such things as interest, downpayment, mortgage payments, balloon payments, and so forth. Two identical properties, at identical prices, may not be equally desirable because of differences in financing terms. On the other hand, by varying terms of a purchase, a property that might otherwise be undesirable could become a good investment, compatible with your goals.

Location

There is an old standard rule of thumb in the real estate investment business. That rule is, "The three most important factors in evaluating investment properties are location, location, and location." While this may largely be true, desirable locations for properties can differ with differing investment goals, resources, investment attitudes, and other considerations. Remember that what may be a totally unacceptable property for one investor, because of its location, may turn out to be another investor's gold mine. Also, desirable locations change over time. Witness the changes that have occurred in some large inner city areas.

Investor's available resources

An investor's resources include his or her time, talent, money, and contacts. Even if a property is being offered at a very low price, if it needs work and the investor doesn't have the adequate resources to repair or maintain it, then he or she should look elsewhere. On the other hand, with the right combination of resources, some properties that otherwise might be unwise investments may be highly desirable. Don't overlook the value of the right contacts. Good plumbers, electricians, carpenters, roofers, wholesalers, and bankers can be of great assistance to the real estate investor when his own time, talent, or money may not be adequate for a particular investment.

Probably the most important resource for the investor is money. It is ridiculous for investors to try to purchase property they cannot afford. Too many real estate writers, salesmen, and consultants are trying to convince uninformed investors to buy property they cannot afford. By misusing creative financing methods, many investors are placing themselves in extremely risky positions that could jeopardize their financial futures for many years. While it is possible to get into real estate investment with relatively little money, the investor must be extremely careful and coldly objective in the evaluation of properties and his or her own resources.

Property income statement

In the final analysis of any property, its success or failure rests upon the numbers. It is a shame that this aspect of property evaluation is so often neglected. In addition, when many investors do make an effort to analyze a property's income, they simply subtract their monthly mortgage, taxes, and insurance payment from any income generated from the property. This simple calculation can be greatly deceiving. The National Association of Realtors has published a much more realistic property income statement that can be invaluable in investment property selection.

Personality of the investor

Some investors are more averse to risk than others. This key personality trait will largely determine the nature of their investment goals, even if they are unaware of how important it is in evaluating properties. By recognizing the importance of this trait, many investors can avoid unnecessary stress and concentrate on properties compatible with their personalities. For example, some properties are very risky, even though there may be a possibility of a high payoff in the end. An example would be a condemned building that the investors hope to improve so that the condemnation will be lifted, thereby greatly increasing the value and salability of the property. This kind of property is not generally advisable for risk-averse persons who should limit their purchase to less risky investments.

Condition of the property

It is a commonly known fact that condition is a major factor in property selection. Consideration of the condition, however, goes much further than mere appearance. Investors must consider many factors which may or may not be visible. Cosmetic blemishes generally can be fixed at relatively low cost. Structural problems are more serious and costly. Most investors shy away from property with severe structural damage unless other considerations overwhelmingly compensate for the repair costs. If you have questions about which problems are cosmetic and which are structural be sure to have an expert appraise the problem before any final decision is made about whether to buy. Other elements affecting a property may not have anything to do with its physical condition. Such things as liens and judgments against properties also are conditions that can greatly affect their desirability. A thorough title search is a prerequisite for any real estate purchase.

Design

In general, standard designs with standard floor plans are more marketable to more people than are nonstandard designs and floor plans. While an eccentric design may perfectly suit one individual, that same design may turn into a white elephant for the investor. One example might be something that looks like a castle in the middle of an otherwise conservative middle class residential area. Nonstandard floor plans would include such things as having access to living area parts of a home only through the master bedroom, the front door opening directly into the kitchen, or no provision for a dining area. The problems with nonstandard designs are: (1) they cannot be changed, except at great expense; and (2) it may be very difficult to find a buyer or tenant.

Comparison with other properties

Most investors compare various aspects of different properties before making a decision to buy. The different kinds of comparisons include properties in the neighborhood, similar properties that recently have been sold, and similar properties currently for sale.

In a comparison of other properties in the neighborhood, as a general rule, investors try to make sure they are not buying the nicest, most expensive home on a street, because the people who could afford to buy that home probably will be attracted to a more exclusive neighborhood. Consequently, either the home will become difficult to sell or its price will have to be reduced so much that very little if any profit is realized from the investment. Comparison of properties that have sold most recently gives the investor a reasonable price range for the prospective property. By comparing properties that are currently for sale, the investor can evaluate other investment opportunities. It is important to remember that every item in a comparison should be reflected in the price of a property. For example, if an investor is comparing two duplexes, and one duplex is located on a busy street and another is located in a more secluded area, then the busy street probably is going to decrease the value of the one in comparison to the other. Numbers and sizes of rooms, age, amenities, location, construction design, and other factors all may be compared to determine the fair prices of different properties.

Introduction to creative financing

You have read and heard a lot about *creative financing* techniques and how they can make you rich in real estate. You need to know that there is a great deal more to the story. These same techniques that are being touted as everybody's road to riches can threaten your financial security for years. Not that creative financing is bad, but rather, you must understand its dangers as well as its promise.

Many books, articles, and seminars promise easy wealth in the real estate business using these methods. Many people are reading these books and then diving into investments with little added information. What these books fail to point out is that it is also possible for real estate investors to lose time, money, home, property, and even their freedom. The dangers are even greater at such times as these, when

2

high interest rates have prohibited conventional financing, forcing property owners to agree to some sort of creative financing arrangements in order to sell their property. This "creative" deal oftentimes is not in the best interest of either party involved.

The information contained in this book is valuable to anyone buying or selling a home. That includes both professional investors and home owners who may not think of their homes as business investments. Although a person may not specifically be interested in becoming an "investor" as such, it is important to be careful in these transactions, simply because so much money is involved. The amount is generally a large portion of the total wealth of the individual or family.

A few short case histories may help illustrate the two sides of this coin. The following six scenarios describe actual situations involving real people. Each case illustrates different

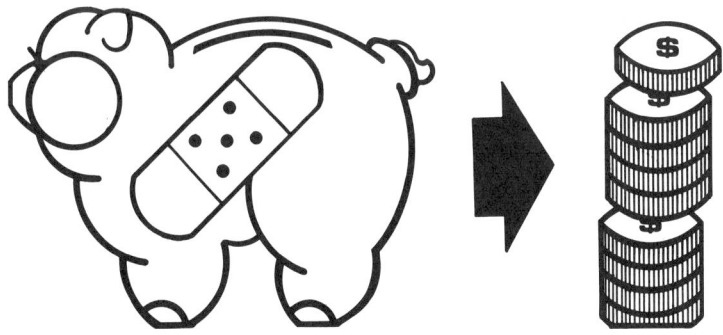

Rags to riches and back again

principles, which are discussed after each scenario. You need to understand that these principles are important basics for any home owner or real estate investor. While they are not everything you need to know, they are very important.

Case 1

An 18-year-old youth, who recently had been graduated from high school, watched his friends spend their money for cars and good times. He decided that he would rather invest his money. Members of his family had successfuly invested in real estate property, and, taking their lead, he spent $1,000 of his own money and borrowed an additional $7,000 for the down payment on a duplex. He signed a 30-year contract with the owner for $33,500. He rented the property for two and one-half years and then sold it for $66,000. Figuring the price of the property, rent collected, interest charges, taxes, minor repairs, and maintenance, he converted his original $1,000 out of pocket cash into more than $25,000 profit before taxes.

Principles

The critical factor to the youth's success in this case was his reliance upon other people that were knowledgeable in real estate. He realized his inexperience and sought the help of someone more experienced in such investments. The same principle applies to anyone needing help, regardless of background. If you are inexperienced in a particular type of transaction, it may be wise to seek out the help of a person who has had more experience in that area. The other important principles that governed the success of the investment can be outlined as follows:

- The property was located in a desirable residential area with high demand.
- The sale price and the financing arrangements were

made so that the rental income from the property would cover mortgage payments and all expenses.

Conservative real estate investors restrict their purchases to property that can pay for itself. That means having a positive cash flow, or at least a break-even operation. The factors that contributed to positive cash flows in the first case were

1. a purchase price no more than fair market value of the property
2. favorable interest rates
3. good rental income because of the high demand for housing
4. good management and maintenance of the property.

We will discuss later and in more depth this principle of positive cash flow.

The investor *shopped* the property carefully before he bought it. *Shopping* here means simply doing your homework. For example, comparing prices in different neighborhoods for comparable properties and determining appropriate rents for housing in the area.

The investor improved the property so that he rented and later sold it in better condition than he had bought it. The point is not to improve for improvement's sake, but rather to increase the profitability of the property through improvements. Improvements generally are worth more to renters or new buyers than the expenditures to make the improvements.

By selling to the new buyer with conventional financing, the investor received the total sales price at the time of sale. The new buyer borrowed the money from a financing institution and paid the full price when he purchased the property. Had the new buyer financed the property with the seller, then the seller would have received payments in monthly installments over future years. While there are circumstances where this type of owner financing is appropriate, the safest sale is always for cash, either cash from the buyer's own resources or from a conventional type loan. We also discuss this principle later in detail.

A final point needs to be made. At the time of the transactions described in case 1, the economy was strong and growing so that the risks often associated with such an investment were minimized.

Case 2

More than 20 years ago an investor, then in his forties, bought a variety store and a new home at the same time. After a couple of years he was having trouble in the variety store business, but sold his house for a $3,000 profit. This sale convinced him that he could make more money easier in buying and selling homes than in selling variety goods. He sold the store and began a real estate business. His objectives were to earn a high monthly income and build a solid retirement. His strategy since then has been to buy houses directly from the owners with a substantial down payment with the seller carrying the remaining balance on an installment contract. He then sells the homes at a profit with a slightly higher interest rate than he has to pay. He sells the houses to families who have money enough only for very small down payments and then finances the houses himself. Interestingly, he never buys a house until he has a buyer. He finds a buyer who doesn't have enough cash for the usual down payment and then shops with the buyer for the house. This strategy earns him a substantial profit each year and enables him to accomplish his objectives of high monthly income and retirement savings.

Principles

The principle key to this investor's success is his refusal to speculate on real estate. He carries no inventory since each property is sold before he buys it. Another contributing factor to his success is an open, candid relationship with his clients so that they understand the total arrangement. In fact, they usually seek him out because of his reputation. They understand that he makes a fair profit, but also they understand that they are able to buy a home that they otherwise could not afford with their limited cash.

A third factor is his diligent management of the various properties. His personal contact with his buyers and regular visits to the different homes serve as incentive for buyers to make prompt payments.

Finally, by buying only from owners willing to finance their own properties (called "owner financing" or "buying on contract"), he is able to finance property at much lower interest rates than he would have to pay using conventional financing. By financing properties himself when he sells them, he can still sell them at lower interest rates to his buyers than they would have to pay at a bank or savings and loan, even after he adds interest for his profit.

Case 3

Another investor bought two small apartment complexes and six months later sold one of them for about $20,000 profit. Following this and other profitable property investments, he told one of his friends that the key to his success was the ease in which he was able to finance the purchases with the sellers on installment contracts. He did not have to meet stringent bank qualifications for loans to purchase the properties because the sellers themselves would extend the credit he needed for the amount he owed. As he expanded his holdings he began attracting silent partners to make the down payments on new properties in exchange for joint ventures. As his financial success increased, he expanded into other businesses as well as real estate, but alway concentrated his energies in the properties.

Eventually he bought an apartment complex of more than 100 units in another state. He convinced the seller to transfer him the title, free and clear, before he paid any money for the property at all, with the promise that he would pay the down payment as soon as he could make the proper bank arrangements in his home state. The investor borrowed heavily against the new property, paid the required down-payment for the building and used the rest of the money for expenses in his non-real estate businesses. He later defaulted on both loans—the one to the seller of the apartment complex and the other to the bank. He was eventually jailed for fraud.

He also had borrowed against his other properties from multiple sources and later filed for bankruptcy with more than $5 million in debt. He recently disappeared from a minimum security correctional facility and had not been found at the time of the writing of this book. The seller of the apartment complex and the others involved in his real estate transactions have suffered great financial losses.

Principles

This case offers insights into the factors contributing to the investor's early success, later downfall, and the failures associated with those people doing business with him.

The investor's early success can be attributed primarily to the use of creative financing techniques, such as little or no money down on large properties that he could resell at substantial profits. He picked the properties carefully. The point was to buy properties that could be resold easily, providing him the profits. The creative financing arrangements allowed him to make the purchases. We should note that the growing economy, with rapidly rising real estate prices, also contributed to his ability to turn over properties quickly at relatively large profits. A weaker economy would not have produced such rapid gains in wealth.

The main factors leading to his downfall can be outlined as follows: By overusing creative financing techniques, he overextended his ability to pay his debts. He simply borrowed more money than his investments could pay for. He then used the dangerous strategy of refinancing properties simply to raise cash to keep afloat, without reinvesting the money from the new loans in new profitable ventures. Finally, a major character flaw, dishonesty, overcame him.

The investor was not alone in the unfortunate consequences of this case. First, the silent partners entering joint ventures with him lost much of their investments. Plus, the woman who sold him the large apartment complex in an adjacent state lost a small fortune. She sold a multimillion dollar building to the investor, who paid her only a small down payment and who then borrowed heavily against it. Although she did get the building back, she had to repay approximately half a million dollars in loans that the buyer had made against it.

The failures that others experienced in this particular real estate investment resulted primarily from the failure to verify the credibility of the investor and the risks associated of doing business with him. Of course, the woman committed a major business blunder by giving him a free and clear title without any payment at all.

Case 4

One young woman invested her savings in a new home, signing a contract with the owner for relatively low monthly payments and for a large balloon payment for the unpaid balance of the loan at the end of two years. In order to buy the home she felt she had to agree to the balloon payment, and she received assurances that it was a wise investment. The purchase was made at a time of rising interest costs, and many in the real estate and financial community expected the rates to fall as the economy strengthened. She believed that after the interest rates went down, she could refinance the home at the new lower rates. Instead of going down, however, the interest rates rose even higher, and after two years she was neither able to pay the amount of the balloon nor able to refinance the balance. She lost the house, her savings used for the down payment, and all equity in the house. She is now renting an apartment.

Principles

One of the first lessons successful real estate investors learn is that there should be no emotional attachment to any investment property. In this case the buyer was purchasing a home, not necessarily investment property. Home buyers normally develop an attachment to their houses, but even then, that attachment must not become so strong that it overwhelms good judgment. When it does happen that a buyer becomes too emotionally attached to a property, the tendency is to agree to unfavorable terms in the purchase agreement. No property is worth unacceptable business or financial risks. The young woman made this common error. She wanted the house so badly that she was willing to make a very unwise decision to get it.

Two major problems should have been apparent in evaluating the decision to purchase the property. First, she was risking her savings on speculation of future economic factors outside her control. There was no real assurance, despite what she was told, that the interest rates would fall, which would have enabled her to refinance the property in order to pay the balloon. As it turned out, interest rates increased instead.

Second, balloon payments are very risky unless the investor already has the resources to pay them when the contract is made. For example, an investor might have either cash or an assured later return, such as a bond that will mature. Too many buyers contract for balloon payments without knowing how, or if, they can acquire the money when it comes due. The nature of financing with balloon payments and their associated problems are so important that we have devoted extensive attention to them in chapter 5.

Case 5

Another individual getting started in real estate bought a small apartment building and financed it with the previous owners of the complex. The monthly payments were about $1,800, which were more than covered by the rents collected from the tenants. The investor sold the building on an installment sale at a substantial profit with payments contracted at $2,400 per month. He did not check the credit on the buyer, who already was highly leveraged (that is, deep in debt in other investments). Shortly after the building was sold, the buyer failed to continue payments. A court suit followed, and for more than three months, the investor was responsible for his $1,800 monthly payments without the rental income from the building or the contracted payments from the new owner. He was forced to sell other assets at substantial losses to raise the amount of his payments. Although the suit was settled satisfactorily out of court, the investor experienced significant losses on other assets, and he lost additional investment opportunities because of his money and energy tied up in the suit.

Principles

Several factors combined to make this property a major headache for the investor. He financed the property himself on contract to a buyer who already was deep in dept. The property produced a negative cash flow for the new buyer, which meant that the rental income did not cover the new buyer's mortgage and other expenses of owning the building. The new buyer had to make up the difference out of his other income. The negative cash flow from the building put additional strains on the new buyer's pocketbook.

    Remember that the seller was still making payments on the building after the sale since he sold the building on contract to the new buyer. Had the building been sold on a conventional loan, he would have received all of his money at the time of sale, which would have enabled him to pay off his loan on the building, relieving him from any further liability. The seller was depending upon the new buyer's payments to cover the payments on his loan of $1,800. Some important principles should be pointed out here. Since the rents from the building did not cover the new buyer's payments to the seller, those payments become dependent upon an additional factor—the buyer's other income. The point is that if the new buyer's other income is inadequate, then he may not be able to pay the difference between the amount of the rents and the payments required for the building. Of course, the new buyer's willingness to make the payments is critical to the success of the investment, and in this case, the main problem arose because the new buyer was unwilling to make the required monthly payments. This factor makes the process of screening prospective buyers extremely important in contract sales. Some sellers even advertise property for sale on contract requiring no qualification or down payment from the buyers. These sellers must anticipate possible problems from such sales.

Case 6

An experienced investor purchased a small house for $24,000. The house had been vacant for almost a year and was in bad repair. The purchase was made on contract with the owner, who had purchased the home himself on contract with the previous owner. This previous owner also had purchased the home on contract from the original owner.

The effect of each new buyer financing the house with each previous owner creates a kind of chain in which every subsequent buyer after the original owner is liable for payments to another member of the chain.

Interestingly, all previous owners have an interest in the property. Should any purchaser default payments, then the member of the chain who had sold the property to that purchaser could take action to recover his loss.

The buyer from the original owner in this case

defaulted. Consequently, the original owner attempted to reclaim the house, jeopardizing the interests of the current investor and the person from whom he bought the home. Because of his experience, however, the current investor knew the applicable laws of the state and all of the members in the ownership chain. When the original owner tried to reclaim the building, the investor reminded her of the legal complications of reclaiming the property and promised her that she would receive payment from him if necessary. The investor then notified all members of the chain of the defaulted payment and applied pressure upon the defaulting person to make payment. By taking these actions the situation was settled satisfactorily for all previous owners, and he avoided losing the property.

Principles

The potential problem in this case was buying into a chain of owner financing. Major problems were avoided by the investor for three reasons:

1. he was familiar with the laws of the state applicable to the business transaction;
2. he made it a point to know all of the members of the buyer chain;
3. he made sure that everyone affected by the default, including the defaulting party, was aware of what was going on.

This free flow of information made the resolution of the problem much easier, less complicated, and more satisfactory than might have been the case for all concerned.

A preview

This chapter has introduced you to the idea that real estate can provide a highly profitable business but a dangerous investment if done badly. The previous cases illustrated this point. The following chapters explain more carefully the nature of real estate financing, advantages and disadvantages of creative financing, potential problems of creative financing, and how to avoid the potential problems. Notice that the emphasis is creative owner financing.

Recent years have produced a trend toward more and more creative owner financing. That being the case, perhaps the primary message you should carry away from this chapter is that "there is no such thing as a free lunch." While creative financing arrangements facilitate the purchase and sale of many properties where conventional financing is difficult to acquire, risks accompany these transactions for both buyer and seller. These risks normally threaten high percentages of the wealth of most investors, since the costs of real estate are high compared to most other investments. The point of the rest of the book is to help you minimize the risks associated with your real estate transactions by being as careful as possible in negotiations and financing arrangements.

Creative financing

Real estate financing arrangements can be classified under two broad headings, *institutional financing* and what many people call *creative financing*. Institutional financing includes things such as conventional loans from banks, savings and loans, and trust companies. The predominant form of creative financing is *owner financing*, where the owner of a property contracts with the buyer for future installment payments to be made to the seller instead of to an institution. In effect, the seller rather than a bank or other institution is lending the money to the buyer. The main difference to the seller can be outlined as follows: If the buyer receives institutional financing, the seller receives all of the sales price at the time of sale from the lending institution. The buyer then pays the lending institution periodic installments on the loan over

3

future years. On the other hand, if the seller finances the property, the seller does not receive the total purchase price at the time of the sale; but rather, the sales price, along with interest, is received in the future installments. When selling on contract the seller retains title to the property until the contract is paid in full, but the buyer obtains possession at the time of sale (i.e., ownership rights). Of course, the seller must pay off any outstanding loans he has made on the property before acquiring the title himself. The amount of the loan in both methods of financing, institutional and creative, is the price of the property minus any down payment. Let's consider some examples of these different financing arrangements.

Call it: heads or tails

Real estate financing

Institutional financing

Suppose a person buys a duplex for $100,000, makes a $20,000 down payment, and finances the balance with a bank at 15% interest over 30 years. This is a conventional mortgage made by the buyer with the bank. The seller receives all $100,000. He receives $20,000 from the buyer and $80,000 from the bank at the time of sale. The distinguishing characteristic of institutional financing is that the buyer makes payments directly to the bank on the $80,000 mortgage. The same type of scenario could be made for any residential property.

Creative financing

Suppose the buyer in the previous example paid $20,000 down directly to the seller, who owned the property free and clear. Suppose further that the buyer contracts with the seller to pay the remaining $80,000 at 12% interest over the following 25 years in monthly payments. This arrangement is a simple "contract sale."

If the seller had not owned the property free and clear, but was still paying on his mortgage, then the financing becomes slightly more complex. Let's examine two cases, one where the buyer assumes the seller's loan and one where the buyer does not.

In both examples, assume the seller still owes $45,000 on the property and is currently making monthly payments of $400. In the first case, the buyer assumes the liability of the seller's $45,000 loan, and the seller is released from all related obligations. The buyer pays the $400 monthly payments to the person or institution who lent the money, assuming the terms remain the same. The buyer and seller sign an additional contract for the remaining $35,000 balance at 12% interest for 30 years, whereby the buyer pays the seller $360 a month. Notice that the interest rates on the two elements of the total payment are not necessarily the same. The seller and buyer may negotiate the interest rate on the $35,000 independently of the seller's original mortgage. The buyer's total monthly payment, then, is $760 ($400 on the assumed loan and $360 directly to the seller). In this case, we say that the seller has taken a "second mortgage" on the property.

In the second case, suppose after making the $20,000 down payment that the buyer contracts to pay the seller all $80,000 at 12% interest for 30 years. Briefly, a seller's "wrap-around contract" occurs when the seller still owes a mortgage on the property being sold and the buyer does not assume or pay off the balance of the seller's loan. The buyer is paying the seller for both the seller's equity in the property and for the balance of the seller's loan. This contract between the buyer and the seller in effect covers (i.e., wraps around) both the seller's loan and equity in the property. This effect of a wrap-around contract is diagrammed below and contrasted with an assumption contract. This arrangement requires the buyer to pay $822 monthly. The seller is still liable for the $400 monthly payments on his mortgage. He has a $422 ($822 minus $400) monthly cash inflow after making that payment. This special case of owner financing is called a seller's wrap-around contract.

In order for an investor to conduct the forementioned simple transactions, he must first familiarize himself with the necessary legal documents. Two of the most basic documents are illustrated in the following section.

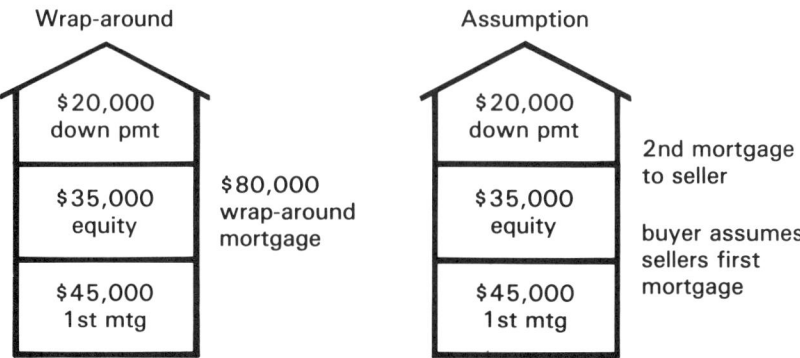

Real estate contracts

There are many documents that may be associated with purchases and sales of real estate property, but a few are most prevalent. Also, you should remember that the forms of the documents change from state to state. They do, however, have some general characteristics in common across states. The following descriptions of two important documents will help you understand more about the nature of the actual transaction once the decision to buy or sell has been made.

Offer to purchase and earnest money

The offer to purchase is the first formal contract between the buyer and the seller. It formalizes the buyer's offer to buy a property. A second contract, the earnest money agreement along with a check or cash is presented to the seller, indicating the buyer's serious intent. This offer to purchase and earnest money constitute a preliminary agreement from which the final contract is drawn. (See p. 30 for a sample form—this one is used by the Utah Department of Business Regulation.)

A major problem with offer-to-purchase contracts is that they usually are written on a standard form that too often does not fit the final sales agreement. Many of the standard forms used across the country were designed when conventional financing was predominant. The wave of "creative" owner financing, with its many variations, has changed the nature of the final contract used to the extent that the traditional offer-to-purchase contract doesn't conform to all of the newer creative provisions of the sale. While this shortcoming can be overcome, many offers to purchase are written simply by the "paint-by-the-number syndrome." This means that the standard spaces provided on the contract are filled in until all the blank spaces are completed. That process may appear satisfactory, but when the time comes to close the sale, many questions may remain unanswered in the purchase agreement. Significant misunderstandings may arise to cause a reopening of the negotiations and possible cancellation of the agreement. Typically, some critical information is left off the offer to purchase and earnest-money agreements and the information that is included generally is not specific enough to ensure that there has been a meeting of the minds between the buyer and the seller. Problems can occur on any of the contract items, but those that seem to cause trouble most frequently are taxes, insurance, property inspections, payment structures, and penalties and defaults.

Before pursuing these specific provisions, you need to remember that the earnest-money contract in its standard form in many states represents a three-party agreement among the realtor, the buyer, and the seller. In this case the buyer is required to give the Realtor® earnest money to show his intent at closing. The earnest money is given to the seller as part of the payment. Of course, if the seller were to reject the offer to purchase, then the earnest money would be returned to the would-be buyer. If an agreement is made and the buyer fails to make the purchase, then the entire earnest money generally would be given to the seller for damages suffered.

Now that so many purchases are owner financed and involve only a buyer and seller, the earnest-money/offer-to-purchase contract has become somewhat confusing. The contract now is being used as an agreement binding the buyer to an offer to purchase in a two-party agreement, although it originally was meant as a three-party agreement, with the appropriate statements and provisions in the contract itself. One good reason for including a third party (that is, an agent) to hold the earnest money is to prevent a seller from taking a sizable amount of earnest money from potential buyers and simply leaving town without going through with the sale.

If the seller accepts the buyer's offer, then the seller also signs the contract, which binds the sale until a more formal purchase agreement can be made. The title of this preliminary contract usually includes such terms as "earnest money," "offer to purchase," or "deposit receipt," depending upon the state where the contract is made.

EARNEST MONEY RECEIPT AND OFFER TO PURCHASE

This may be a legally binding form, if not understood seek other advice

TO: _____ Utah, _____ 19 ____
         Name of Broker Company

1.
2. IN CONSIDERATION OF your agreement to use your efforts to present this offer to the Seller, I/we
3. hereby deposit with you as earnest money the sum of ($ _____) _____ DOLLARS
4. in the form of _____
5. to secure and apply on the purchase of the property situated at: _____
6. _____
7. _____
8. _____
9. _____ City _____ County, State of _____
10. including any of the following items if at present attached to the premises: Plumbing and heating fixtures, and equipment including stoker and oil tanks, water heaters, and burners, electric
11. light fixtures excluding bulbs, bathroom fixtures, roller shades, curtain rods and fixtures, venetian blinds, window and door screens, linoleum, all shrubs and trees,   and any other fixtures
12.
13. except _____
14. The following personal property shall also be included as part of the property purchased: _____
15. _____
16. _____
17. The total purchase price of $ (_____) _____ which represents the aforedescribed deposit, receipt of which is hereby acknowledged by you: _____ DOLLARS
18. shall be payable as follows: $ _____
19. $ _____ when seller approves sale: $ _____ on delivery of deed or final contract of
20. sale which shall be on or before _____ 19 _____ , and $ _____ each month commencing
21. _____
22. _____
23. _____
24. _____
25. _____
26. _____
27. until the balance of $ _____ together with interest is paid; provided, however, that buyer at his option, at any time, may pay amounts in excess of the monthly
28. payments upon the unpaid balance, subject to the limitations of any mortgage or contract by the buyer herein assumed. Interest at _____ % per annum on the unpaid portions of the
29. purchase price to be included in the prescribed payments and shall begin as of date of possession which shall be on or before _____ 19 _____ . All risk of loss and destruction

30 of property, and expenses of insurance shall be born by the seller until date of possession at which time property taxes, rents, insurance, interest and other expenses of the property shall be
31 prorated as of date of possession. All other taxes and all assessments, mortgages, chattel liens and other liens, encumbrances or charges against the property of any nature shall be paid by
the seller except: _____

32 The following special improvements are included in this sale: Sewer ☐ —Connected ☐ , Septic Tank and/or Cesspool ☐ , Sidewalk ☐ , Curb and Gutter ☐ , Special Street Paving
33 ☐ , Special Street Lighting ☐ , Culinary Water (City ☐ , Other Community System ☐ , Private ☐ .) (Legend: Yes (x) No (o).
34
35 Contract of Sale or Instrument of conveyance to be made on the approved form of the Utah Dept. of Business Regulation in the name of

36 _____

37 This payment is received and offer is made subject to the written acceptance of the seller endorsed hereon within _____ days from date hereof, and unless so
38 approved the return of the money herein receipted shall cancel this offer without damage to the undersigned agent.

39 In the event the purchaser fails to pay the balance of said purchase price or complete said purchase as herein provided, the amounts paid hereon shall, at the option of the seller,
40 be retained as liquidated and agreed damages.

41 It is understood and agreed that the terms written in this receipt constitute the entire Preliminary Contract between the purchaser and the seller, and that no verbal statement made by
42 anyone relative to this transaction shall be construed to be a part of this transaction unless incorporated in writing herein. It is further agreed that execution of the final contract shall
43 abrogate this Earnest Money Receipt and Offer to Purchase.

44 _____ Agent By _____
        Broker Company

45 We do hereby agree to carry out and fulfill the terms and conditions specified above, and the seller agrees to furnish good and marketable title with abstract brought to date or at Seller's
46 option a policy of title insurance in the name of the purchaser and to make final conveyance by warranty deed or _____ ;
47 in the event of sale of other than real property, seller will provide evidence of title or right to sell or lease. If either party fails so to do, he agrees to pay all expenses of enforcing this agree-
48 ment, or of any right arising out of the breach thereof, including a reasonable attorney's fee.
49 The seller agrees in consideration of the efforts of the agent in procuring a purchaser, to pay said agent a commission of _____
50 In the event seller has entered into a listing contract with any other agent and said contract is presently effective, this paragraph will be of no force or effect.

51 _____   _____
        Date   Seller

52 _____   _____
        Date   Seller

RECEIPT

53 (State law requires brokers to furnish copies of this contract bearing all signatures to buyer and seller. Dependent upon the method used, one of the following forms must be completed.)
54 I acknowledge receipt of a final copy of the foregoing agreement bearing all signatures:

55 _____   _____   _____
        Seller   Date   Purchaser   Date

56 I personally caused a final copy of the foregoing agreement bearing all signatures to be mailed to the ☐ Seller, ☐ Purchaser, on
57 _____ 19 _____ , by registered mail and return receipt is attached hereto.

58 Broker _____ By _____

You as buyer or seller must be careful to include in the offer to purchase and earnest-money contracts *all* of the provisions that you want in the final contract. This practice helps avoid unpleasant surprises at the final signing, at which time it is not uncommon for a buyer and seller to be forced to resume negotiations on items that were not well-defined in the earlier offer to buy.

Also, remember that the earnest money is a tool to be used by the buyer or investor. For example, if you are making several offers within a short period of time, it may be advisable to include as little earnest money as possible. Since every offer requires earnest money, by including as little as possible the investor avoids obligating unnecessary amounts of cash at once. On the other hand, if you know that other offers are being made on a property and it is important to you to buy it, then it may help to increase the earnest money in order to convince the seller that you are the most capable buyer.

For example, two offers were made on a duplex for $100,000. The only difference was that one offer included $100 earnest money and the other offer included $2,000 earnest money. The second offer was more attractive and was accepted, because it represented greater security to the seller should anything happen to stop the sale.

As a general rule, sellers should require larger amounts of earnest money to compensate their time and inconvenience if a buyer defaults. It is not uncommon for the seller to receive other offers after setting a closing date with one buyer. This means that each additional potential buyer was declined, and the property was taken off the market, because of the good faith relationship based upon the earnest-money contract. This waiting period between signing an earnest money contract and the closing date usually is between 30 and 60 days. This period is called the "time under contract." Often times there is no indication before the last day that the buyer will not consummate the purchase. In that case, a small amount of earnest money may not compensate for the time and energy spent and also for the probable loss of another buyer.

Three remedies to this problem are:

1. to require more earnest money
2. to accept back-up offers from other potential buyers
3. to maintain contact with other interested parties during the time under contract.

The final agreement

The final sales contract (see page 34 for a sample form, this one from the State of Utah) supercedes any previous verbal or written temporary agreement between the buyer and the seller. It outlines the conditions of sale agreed upon by the buyer and the seller and should act as the final word in any disputed claims by either party. Unfortunately, it shares some of the same problems that the offer to purchase has. It suffers from the same "paint-by-the-number syndrome." Many of its provisions are open for dispute because either

1. they are not covered in the contract or
2. they are unclear as the standard contract is written

Specific problems can arise over such things as forfeiture and foreclosure, taxes, insurance, property inspection, payment structures, penalties and defaults, delivery of deed and title insurance. Too often these provisions either are ignored or are inadequately outlined so that subsequent problems can occur between the buyer and the seller. These problems are so important to the purchase and sales transaction that we have devoted several of the remaining chapters to them, outlining them with their remedies.

"THIS IS A LEGALLY BINDING CONTRACT. IF NOT UNDERSTOOD, SEEK COMPETENT ADVICE."

UNIFORM REAL ESTATE CONTRACT

1. THIS AGREEMENT, made in duplicate this _____ day of _____, A. D., 19____,
by and between _____
hereinafter designated as the Seller, and _____

hereinafter designated as the Buyer, of _____

2. WITNESSETH: That the Seller, for the consideration herein mentioned agrees to sell and convey to the buyer, and the buyer for the consideration herein mentioned agrees to purchase the following described real property, situate in the county of _____, State of Utah, to-wit: _____
ADDRESS
More particularly described as follows:

3. Said Buyer hereby agrees to enter into possession and pay for said described premises the sum of _____ Dollars ($_____)
payable at the office of Seller, his assigns or order _____
strictly within the following times, to-wit: _____ ($_____)
cash, the receipt of which is hereby acknowledged, and the balance of $_____ shall be paid as follows:

Possession of said premises shall be delivered to buyer on the _____ day of _____, 19____.

4. Said monthly payments are to be applied first to the payment of interest and second to the reduction of the principal. Interest shall be charged from _____ on all unpaid portions of the purchase price at the rate of _____ per cent (_____%) per annum. The Buyer, at his option at anytime, may pay amounts in excess of the monthly payments upon the unpaid balance subject to the limitations of any mortgage or contract by the Buyer herein assumed, such excess to be applied either to unpaid principal or in prepayment of future installments at the election of the buyer, which election must be made at the time the excess payment is made.

5. It is understood and agreed that if the Seller accepts payment from the Buyer on this contract less than according to the terms herein mentioned, then by so doing, it will in no way alter the terms of the contract as to the forfeiture hereinafter stipulated, or as to any other remedies of the seller.

6. It is understood that there presently exists an obligation against said property in favor of _____ with an unpaid balance of $_____, as of _____.

7. Seller represents that there are no unpaid special improvement district taxes covering improvements to said premises now in the process of being installed, or which have been completed and not paid for, outstanding against said property, except the following _____

8. The Seller is given the option to secure, execute and maintain loans secured by said property of not to exceed the then unpaid contract balance hereunder, bearing interest at the rate of not to exceed _____ percent (_____%) per annum and payable in regular monthly installments; provided that the aggregate monthly installment payments required to be made by Seller on said loans shall not be greater than each installment payment required to be made by the Buyer under this contract. When the principal due hereunder has been reduced to the amount of any such loans and mortgages the Seller agrees to convey and the Buyer agrees to accept title to the above described property subject to said loans and mortgages.

9. If the Buyer desires to exercise his right through accelerated payments under this agreement to pay off any obligations outstanding at date of this agreement against said property, it shall be the Buyer's obligation to assume and pay any penalty which may be required on prepayment of said prior obligations. Prepayment penalties in respect to obligations against said property incurred by seller, after date of this agreement, shall be paid by seller unless said obligations are assumed or approved by buyer.

10. The Buyer agrees upon written request of the Seller to make application to a reliable lender for a loan of such amount as can be secured under the regulations of said lender and hereby agrees to apply any amount so received upon the purchase price above mentioned, and to execute the papers required and pay one-half the expenses necessary in obtaining said loan, the Seller agreeing to pay the other one-half, provided however, that the monthly payments and interest rate required, shall not exceed the monthly payments and interest rate as outlined above.

11. The Buyer agrees to pay all taxes and assessments of every kind and nature which are or which may be assessed and which may become due on these premises during the life of this agreement. The Seller hereby covenants and agrees that there are no assessments against said premises except the following:

The Seller further covenants and agrees that he will not default in the payment of his obligations against said property.

12. The Buyer agrees to pay the general taxes after _____

13. The Buyer further agrees to keep all insurable buildings and improvements on said premises insured in a company acceptable to the Seller in the amount of not less than the unpaid balance on this contract, or $_____ and to assign said insurance to the Seller as his interests may appear and to deliver the insurance policy to him.

14. In the event the Buyer shall default in the payment of any special or general taxes, assessments or insurance premiums as herein provided, the Seller may, at his option, pay said taxes, assessments and insurance premiums or either of them, and if Seller elects so to do, then the Buyer agrees to repay the Seller upon demand, all such sums so advanced and paid by him, together with interest thereon from date of payment of said sums at the rate of ¾ of one percent per month until paid.

15. Buyer agrees that he will not commit or suffer to be committed any waste, spoil, or destruction in or upon said premises, and that he will maintain said premises in good condition.

16. In the event of a failure to comply with the terms hereof by the Buyer, or upon failure of the Buyer to make any payment or payments when the same shall become due, or within _____ days thereafter, the Seller, at his option shall have the following alternative remedies:

    A. Seller shall have the right, upon failure of the Buyer to remedy the default within five days after written notice, to be released from all obligations in law and in equity to convey said property, and all payments which have been made theretofore on this contract by the Buyer, shall be forfeited to the Seller as liquidated damages for the non-performance of the contract, and the Buyer agrees that the Seller may at his option re-enter and take possession of said premises without legal processes as in its first and former estate, together with all improvements and additions made by the Buyer thereon, and the said additions and improvements shall remain with the land become the property of the Seller, the Buyer becoming at once a tenant at will of the Seller; or

    B. The Seller may bring suit and recover judgment for all delinquent installments, including costs and attorneys fees. (The use of this remedy on one or more occasions shall not prevent the Seller, at his option, from resorting to one of the other remedies hereunder in the event of a subsequent default); or

    C. The Seller shall have the right, at his option, and upon written notice to the Buyer, to declare the entire unpaid balance hereunder at once due and payable, and may elect to treat this contract as a note and mortgage, and pass title to the Buyer subject thereto, and proceed immediately to foreclose the same in accordance with the laws of the State of Utah, and have the property sold and the proceeds applied to the payment of the balance owing, including costs and attorney's fees; and the Seller may have a judgment for any deficiency which may remain. In the case of foreclosure, the Seller hereunder, upon the filing of a complaint, shall be immediately entitled to the appointment of a receiver to take possession of said mortgaged property and collect the rents, issues and profits therefrom and apply the same to the payment of the obligation hereunder, or hold the same pursuant to order of the court; and the Seller, upon entry of judgment of foreclosure, shall be entitled to the possession of the said premises during the period of redemption.

17. It is agreed that time is the essence of this agreement.

18. In the event there are any liens or encumbrances against said premises other than those herein provided for or referred to, or in the event any liens or encumbrances other than herein provided for shall hereafter accrue against the same by acts or neglect of the Seller, then the Buyer may, at his option, pay and discharge the same and receive credit on the amount then remaining due hereunder in the amount of any such payment or payments and thereafter the payments herein provided to be made, may, at the option of the Buyer, be suspended until such time as such suspended payments shall equal any sums advanced as aforesaid.

19. The Seller on receiving the payments herein reserved to be paid at the time and in the manner above mentioned agrees to execute and deliver to the Buyer or assigns, a good and sufficient warranty deed conveying the title to the above described premises free and clear of all encumbrances except as herein mentioned and except as may have accrued by or through the acts or neglect of the Buyer, and to furnish at his expense, a policy of title insurance in the amount of the purchase price or at the option of the Seller, an abstract brought to date at time of sale or at any time during the term of this agreement, or at time of delivery of deed, at the option of Buyer.

20. It is hereby expressly understood and agreed by the parties hereto that the Buyer accepts the said property in its present condition and that there are no representations, covenants, or agreements between the parties hereto with reference to said property except as herein specifically set forth or attached hereto _____

21. The Buyer and Seller each agree that should they default in any of the covenants or agreements contained herein, that the defaulting party shall pay all costs and expenses, including a reasonable attorney's fee, which may arise or accrue from enforcing this agreement, or in obtaining possession of the premises covered hereby, or in pursuing any remedy provided hereunder or by the statutes of the State of Utah whether such remedy is pursued by filing a suit or otherwise.

22. It is understood that the stipulations aforesaid are to apply to and bind the heirs, executors, administrators, successors, and assigns of the respective parties hereto.

IN WITNESS WHEREOF, the said parties to this agreement have hereunto signed their names, the day and year first above written.

Signed in the presence of

_____   _____
                                                                                Seller

                                                                    _____
                                                                                Buyer

BLANK NO. 106— GEM PRINTING CO.

Approved Form:

To

Uniform Real Estate Contract

No.

35

Contract chains

Contract selling often is referred to by one of its many names, depending upon the state in which you live—installment sales, wrap-around mortgages, land sales contracts, or more simply, owner financing. In this type of transaction, the owner personally finances the property for the new buyer by taking a contract for the amount owed. The seller retains title to the property, but the buyer obtains possession. After subtracting the down payment from the price of the property, the remainder represents the balance that will be paid to the seller in periodic payments, along with interest. After the total balance has been paid, with any interest, the seller then conveys title to the buyer.

4

When the seller owns a property free and clear—that is, no mortgages are owed—the owner financing can be simple and uncomplicated. If the buyer resells the property before making total payment for the property and before receiving title, a contract chain is created. This chain can grow indefinitely unless otherwise limited by specific provisions in the contracts. Generally, each member of the chain expects to make his or her required payments from the payments received by the next buyer. Here is an example of how chains are created and some of the problems associated with them.

One good thing after another . . . oops!

Alan owns an apartment building and sells it to Bob for $100,000. Bob pays nothing down and contracts monthly payments of $1,000 until the balance and the interest are paid off.

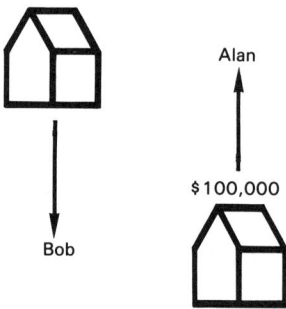

Clair buys the building two years later from Bob for $120,000 with nothing down and monthly payments of $1,300 until the balance and the interest are paid off.

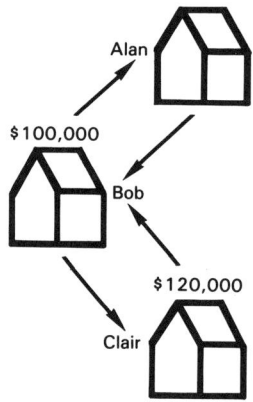

In another three years Clair sells the building to Diane for $150,000 with nothing down and monthly payments of $1,700 until the principal and interest are paid off.

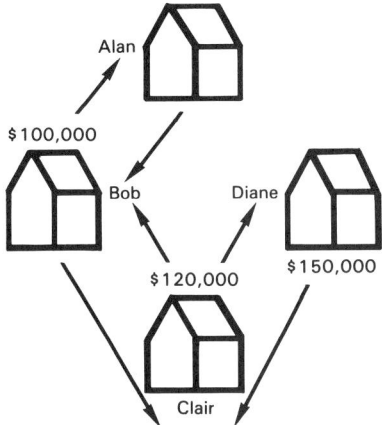

The flow of monthly payments looks like this.

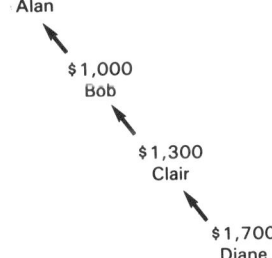

Each time the property is resold, it is financed by the previous owner on an installment sales contract. Alan is the only member of the contract chain with title to the property, but each of the other buyers holds an interest. Each member of the chain will receive title when his or her mortgage is paid off. For example, when Bob pays Alan the total $100,000 plus the required interest, Alan will give him title. The same principle should govern the transfer of title to each subsequent buyer as well.

A major problem can arise with contract chains, however. The following scenario illustrates the problem that can occur when one member of the chain defaults on a contract.

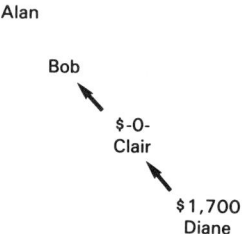

Suppose in the last illustration, for example, that Diane makes her regular payment to Clair, but Clair does not make her monthly payment to Bob. He must then make his payment out of other funds to prevent also going into default. He may not have enough other cash to continue making the payments, especially if Clair remains in default for an extended time. If not, then he likely will go into default along with Clair. Although he does have legal recourse against Clair, by the time he can file for foreclosure, he also likely will be in default to Alan. Consequently, as soon as Bob defaults, Alan may initiate foreclosure proceedings. He has the deed and first claim on the property. Diane is the last person in the chain and may be totally unaware of the defaults. She may find herself in an intricate and expensive lawsuit through no fault of her own. Conceivably she even could lose the property.

In one case, both an individual and a lending institution lost their interest in a property because of problems in the contract chain. An attorney selling his first duplex, sold it on contract to a close friend, who later became short of cash and conveyed his interest in the property to a lending institution. He also illegally sold it to another person. When this buyer tried to sell at a later date, he discovered not only the conflict of interest perpetrated by the individual who had sold him the property, but also the default to the original owner, the attorney. The attorney soon foreclosed on the property, the lending institution lost its interest, and the last buyer, who was trying to sell, also lost his interest in the property. Although he and the lending institution won judgments against the defaulting party, the party in default had no assets, and they were unable to collect anything.

You should remember that even some people whom you might respect as knowledgeable in business do not always understand the workings of some contracts. For example, one CPA who had invested in real estate for several years and who was involved in a contract chain simply did not understand how the chain operated. He believed that when one member of the chain defaulted that the defaulting party was simply removed from the chain and all other members kept positions in the chain, but that the chain was one link shorter. If this were the case, the risk associated with contract chains would diminish greatly. Unfortunately, the CPA was badly misinformed.

Contract chain before default	Incorrect assumption of chain contraction
Original owner First new buyer Second buyer Third buyer	Original owner First new buyer Third buyer

A person in default in a contract chain is not merely circumvented. His action shortens the chain to include only those members above him, not below.

The chain after second party defaults
Original owner First new buyer

As we have shown in the previous example, there is a significant risk in buying into a contract chain. Chains can go into default even after many years. When you sign any contract involving real estate, be sure to have it reviewed by a qualified real estate broker or attorney and be sure to have him explain your rights, obligations, and any risks contained in the contract. Costs for such services are low when compared with what they might be if you were to be surprised with the prospect of a total loss of your investment.

Advantages and disadvantages

Buyer

Although there are certain advantages to buying and selling on contract, there are no distinct advantages to buying into a contract chain that we are aware of. By buying into a chain, a buyer has a very real risk of losing the property.

Seller

By selling in a contract chain, the sellers in high positions risk the loss of contract payments without final rights to the property. The risk is very high when a buyer's payments are necessary for the seller to make payments on a previous contract. The longer the chain, the higher the risk. Plus, once you have sold, you probably have no control over how long the chain can become, unless you make a specific provision in your contract with the new buyer prohibiting a subsequent sale on contract, thereby avoiding the creation of a chain.

How to avoid the problem

The primary objective is to stay out of contract chains. Because of the current market conditions, however, and an abundance of creative financing, any serious home buyer or investor probably will be involved in a chain at sometime. The next best strategy is to employ several devices to diminish the risks.

1. Make a list of all members of the chain and notify them when you buy into it.
2. Have a credit check performed for all members of the chain in front of you as a buyer.
3. If possible, structure the payments when you buy so that you make all of the payments directly to the contract holders in the chain. This avoids another member of the chain taking a payment and then defaulting, jeopardizing your position in the property. While this strategy protects you as the buyer and gives you control over the payments, it is risky to you as a seller, since you then become dependent upon another party to make your payment for you.
4. When you sell on contract, stipulate in the contract that any subsequent sale to be financed either with institutional financing, or if on contract, that the new buyer demonstrate ability to afford the property.
5. In case a default does occur, circumvent that person. Get one or more of the other members of the chain behind that person to make the defaulted payment and then withhold subsequent payments to the defaulting party until that contract is current. Of course, the person withholding payment technically is in default, but this tactic generally keeps the chain alive, prevents foreclosure, and strengthens the person's bargaining position and

that of the other members of the chain when trying to persuade the errant party to make the required payments. Consult an attorney first.
6. Always keep enough cash for at least three or four monthly payments as protection against defaults in the chain.

Balloon payments

A balloon payment is any payment of principal on a loan that is in addition to the regular periodic payments of principal and interest. A balloon payment is applied directly to the principal and reduces the balance of a loan dollar for dollar.

You probably will encounter balloons in both institutional and owner financing. Even though the contracts might appear to operate the same in both institutional and owner financing, the intent of balloon payments and, therefore, the ramifications generally are different in the two different settings.

In the past, institutional lenders used mortgages with balloon payments in order to renegotiate the unpaid balance of loans at the new prevailing rates when the balloon came due. They generally never intended to collect the balloon

5

payment. Rather, they wanted to convert it to a new loan at current interest rates. This method of financing provides a way for financial institutions to protect themselves against inflation. Money lent in 1977, for example, had an interest rate of about 10%. Only four years later, the interest rate was more like 18% or 20%. Outstanding loans at 10% have become unprofitable.

Owners that provide financing for the buyers, however, generally write contracts, including balloon payments, with the sole intent to receive the total payment for a property in a relatively short period of time. This type of contract helps achieve a two-fold goal:

1. sell the property quickly, because it's a contract sale
2. receive the entire sales price in a short period, often as short as one or two years.

The bubble bursts

Also, because the seller is willing to sell on contract with a small down payment and carry the unpaid balance at an interest rate lower than conventional financing, the buyer may be willing to pay an inflated purchase price over and above the true value (see chapter 12). The seller receives a quick sale with quick cash at a high price. To illustrate how balloon payments work, assume you buy a house for $50,000 with nothing down and the seller agrees to carry a three-year contract with 36 monthly payments of $514.31. The payments are based upon 12% interest on a loan amortized for 30 years, even though the contract calls for total payment within three years. This is accomplished with a balloon payment at the end of the 36-month period. Since most of the monthly payments in the early years of a loan go to pay interest, a total of $49,383 in principal remains unpaid at the end of the contract period (3 years). In order to pay off the loan, the total $49,383, would be paid at one time in the form of a balloon payment.

Some contracts call for balloon payments of less than a total unpaid balance. Suppose for example, that the balloon payment were for $20,000 of the unpaid $49,383 balance. A total of $29,383 would remain unpaid at the end of three years. Two different arrangements can be made to pay this remaining balance.

1. You can keep the same payments ($514.31) as before and reduce the number of years left to pay. In this case it would be paid off in seven years.
2. You can reduce the monthly payments of interest and principal. In this case, if you continued to pay based upon 12% interest for 30 years, you would pay $306 a month for the next 27 years.

You should be careful that all balloon payments and their effects on the financing arrangements are explained in detail in the original offer to purchase and in the final contract agreement. Notice from our example that there are at least two choices of handling remaining balances after balloon payments of partial unpaid balances are made. Be sure that the contracts specify how these unpaid balances will be paid. These factors should be negotiated before the sale, because you may want to pay off the property sooner with the current interest rate and the seller may want to revise the interest rate on the remaining balance to be paid over a much longer period. You can either deal with these terms of the contract before the purchase or later, usually at the time of the balloon payment. Sooner is better. Later could be a financial and legal nightmare.

Another problem can occur with balloon payments when a property is sold more than once, each time on contract when a balloon is outstanding. Each time a new contract is written with a balloon payment, the seller usually asks for the "entire unpaid balance" due from the buyer instead of requiring a specific dollar amount. The average seller will not take the time to find out the exact amount of the balloon payment required from his buyer. He purposely asked for a balloon payment in order to raise the money he needs to pay the balloon payment that he agreed to. Not knowing the exact figure can be disastrous as we will see.

To illustrate, an investor purchased a small apartment building on contract that required a balloon payment in 20 years for the entire unpaid balance of $120,000. He sold the property on contract two years later, requiring a balloon payment for the "remaining unpaid balance" due in 18 years, the same date as the balloon payment he had agreed to make. The balloon for that buyer is $166,000. Suppose the property appreciates modestly for the next ten years and is sold again. When the property sells, the owner will most likely require a balloon payment from the new buyer at the end of the 20-year period in order to pay his balloon of $166,000. Assuming again a modest appreciation rate during the years before the sale, a balloon payment for the entire unpaid balance could be well over a half a million dollars at that time.

The original balloon forces subsequent sales to require balloons and the due dates for later balloons will be the same date as for the original balloon payment. That is because each investor will be trying to recover enough from the sale of the property to pay all obligations, including the final balloon payment. They expect that the person to whom they sell will make the required balloon payment which will provide them with cash to pay their balloon. But remember that the debt comes sooner and sooner in subsequent sales. Notice also that with each subsequent sale and as the property appreciates in value, the balloon becomes larger for each new buyer. The consequences of this trend should be almost obvious. The risk of default on later sales becomes quite large, and the marketability of the property also diminishes. In the event of a default on one of the balloon payments, the whole chain of contracts collapses so that no one, including the original owner, receives total payment for the property. One apparent solution might be to refinance the building with an institutional loan, but as the building becomes older, institutional financing is more difficult to acquire. In our example the original balloon is due in 20 years. If the property is 25 years old, it will be 45 years old at the time the balloon payment becomes due. It probably will be very difficult, at best, to acquire refinancing on this property at that time. That would force the use of contract sales the older the building becomes, but as the balloon comes closer on the horizon, the property becomes less and less desirable. Someone will be left with a white elephant he is unable to support. There is a high probability that the ultimate result could be a default on one of the balloons, in which case, everyone in the chain of contracts would suffer a major financial loss on the property. One solution to this problem is to specify the amount of the balloon payment to be the original amount at the end of the final 20-year contract period. In our example, it would be kept at $120,000 with each succeeding sale. The advantage of this strategy is that the balloon does not inflate with each subsequent sale, plus it represents a smaller portion of the total value of the property as it appreciates, which will make refinancing of the amount required for the balloon payment much easier, even from institutional lenders. It is a matter of refinancing $120,000 on a $500,000 building rather than refinancing $400,000 on that same property.

While writing this chapter, the authors received a list of seven homes that were being foreclosed upon because each buyer had defaulted on his particular loan. Of the seven, five included short-term balloon payments. Could these balloons be forcing people to default since there were no possible means by which to refinance? These figures illustrate the frequency with which problems can occur in contracts with balloon payments.

There is a tendency among sellers who sell on contract using balloon payments to assume that they can stop worrying once it sold. In the previous example, the concern may be put off for 20 years by the original buyer, but the danger of significant financial consequences is present from the time the original balloon payment was contracted. As each day passes the investor is one day closer to facing that obligation.

Still another problem with balloon payments is the failure to realize how large they might be. Many buyers will agree to balloon payments in 10, 15, or 20 years because they seem so far into the future. These buyers assume that most of the loan will be paid off by that time. This occurs when buyers do not calculate the amount and they agree to a contract that does not specify the exact amount of the balloon, but rather states simply the "remaining unpaid balance" will be due. The following table illustrates the fallacy of this assumption. The table shows the proportion of the remaining balance of a 30-year loan after 5, 10, 15, and 20 years at four different contract interest rates.

Proportion of original principal still unpaid on 30-year loan

Loan interest rates	Number of years paid on loan			
	5	10	15	20
10%	.96474	.90938	.81664	.66404
12%	.97663	.93427	.85705	.71649
14%	.98430	.95283	.88971	.76312
16%	.98960	.96557	.91561	.80277

Suppose you borrow $75,000 for a house on a 30-year loan at 14%. Using the figures in the table, after 20 years of monthly payments of $888.65, you still will owe more than 76% of the original principle, or $57,234 ($75,000 × .76312). Notice that the great majority of your payments over the 20 years goes to pay interest on the loan. The major part of the loan is paid off in the last few years. In this case more than 50% of the principal will be paid in the last five years of your payments.

A related problem faces the seller of properties who uses creative financing with no money down and a balloon payment due in as little as two years. Notice from our previous discussion that the buyer has paid very little during the two-year period on the principal amount of the loan. By making no down payment and by purchasing only a very small amount of equity in the property in the two years of monthly payments, the buyer becomes strongly tempted to walk away from the property if there are no means to meet the requirements when the balloon comes due. The buyer can then simply consider the payments during that time as rental payments. The buyer may not actually leave the property, forcing the seller to file suit in order to get it back. In that case the legal problems become both tedious and expensive. Most sellers would do better to make a wiser sale in the first place, requiring the buyer to purchase a significant amount of equity in the property before taking possession and by receiving documented assurance that the buyer will be able to meet the balloon payment when it comes due.

Advantages and disadvantages

The primary problem we have discussed is the risk associated with balloon payments. There may be circumstances and considerations however, that would outweigh that risk to the buyer and the seller, so that balloon payments may be advantageous to one or both parties in the contract. Let's examine

Buyer

There are not many occasions when balloon payments are good for buyers. In some circumstances buyers may have a guaranteed income source at a future time. When this situation is the case, then the small monthly payments may allow the buyers to acquire the property with the assurance that they will be able to afford the balloon when it is due. Conservative buyers simply avoid contracts with balloon payments unless they do have assurance at the time of purchase that they will have the required funds to pay any balloons. The problem for the buyer, as we have illustrated, occurs when they do not have such assurance. The risk of not being able to meet the payment is substantial.

Seller

We stated that sellers generally write contracts with balloon payments for the following two reasons:

1. sell the property quickly
2. receive the total payment in a relatively short time

While balloon payments may facilitate the sale of the property, it can be disadvantageous to the seller, simply because of the high risks assumed by the buyer, as we have pointed out. When the seller is assured that a buyer will have sufficient resources to pay any required balloon, then this type of contract is reasonable. Otherwise it is quite dangerous.

How to avoid the problem

Buyers and sellers simply should not contract for balloon payments unless the buyer is assured of adequate resources when the contract is signed to pay any required balloons. As we have pointed out, expectations of refinancing the balloon payment or of reselling the property are not adequate assurance that the resources will be available. The buyer needs the assets at the purchase date either in the form of cash or cash equivalents, such as bonds, stocks, certificates of deposit, and so forth. Even then, these assets may not be available when the balloon comes due, because they may be required for other investments in the meantime.

Negative cash flows

We mentioned that negative cash flows occur when the revenues from a property are less than the expenditures required to own and operate the property. This situation can pose significant problems for both buyers and sellers of such properties. The following case illustrates this point.

An investor sold a duplex to a partnership for $128,000. The partnership paid $38,000 down for the property and contracted to pay the rest to the seller in $700 installments over 30 years. The property generated only slightly more than $500 gross income per month to the new owners. These rents failed to cover the monthly contract payments, much less the other ownership costs, such as taxes, insurance, maintenance, repairs, and utilities. Another important cost is the vacancy factor. The total negative cash flow to the buyers was

6

approximately $400 per month. Simply, that means that every month the buyers had to spend $400 more for the property than they were collecting. The buyers made the contract in the expectation that the property value would increase substantially so that when they sold it, the rapid increase in value would compensate the negative cash flows. Their major interest in the property was the land, which typically does increase in value. As it turned out, three years after the building and land had been sold, the appraised value of the property was much less than had been expected. The fact that the value of the property failed to meet the partnership's expectations forced it to keep the property in continued hopes of future appreciation. In the meantime, the negative cash flow represented almost $5,000 per year additional cash investment in the property that had to be recouped if the new owners were to be able to break even, much less make a profit.

Caught in quicksand

Also, the negative cash flow put a strain on the buyer's other income. Sellers of such properties are in a very risky position, because as we pointed out in chapter 1, *the contract payments do not depend solely upon the property's income, but also upon the buyer's other income sources.*

Advantages and disadvantages

The above case illustrates the impact of negative cash flows on an investment. Despite these problems, however, there are occasions when both the buyer and the seller may have good reason to enter into a contract involving negative cash flows from a property. Let's examine the reasons why a buyer would or would not want to invest in a property producing negative cash flows.

Buyer

There are occasions when a well-informed investor might decide to purchase a property with a negative cash flow. Three occasions follow:

1. The property has a high probability of rapidly increasing in value enough to compensate the negative cash flows upon its resale.
2. The property may serve as a tax shelter.
3. The investor believes that the income from the property can be increased enough to generate positive cash flows.

A combination of these circumstances may also occur.

In any of these three events, the investor must be able to afford the negative cash flow. That means that the investor must be able to generate enough cash from other resources on a regular basis to meet cash obligations required by the property. Because of the risks resulting from negative cash flows, this investment strategy should be limited to those investors who can afford to continue unexpected cash outlays for indefinite periods when things go wrong. Notice, for example, that the partnership's expectation of rapidly increasing property value did not occur in the above case. The investors then had to hold the property much longer than they planned.

The major disadvantage of *investing in negative cash flow property is that the risk goes beyond the property itself to include other resources.* A series of bad investments in negative cash flow properties can destroy an investor financially.

Seller

The advantage to the seller would appear to be the same as that for any property. A negative cash flow property can be sold to generate regular income since the buyer's mortgage payments to the seller are often greater than the rent the seller was collecting. Of course, as we pointed out, when a buyer becomes unable to support negative cash flows, then the seller suffers. In effect, the buyer's risk is passed on to the seller, so that they both share in the risk of negative cash flows. Even though the seller can generally repossess the property, this action is seldom ideal and may result in some sort of financial loss.

How to avoid the problem

The surest way to avoid the problems of properties generating negative cash flows is simply to avoid those properties. Interestingly, sometimes a property that appears to have a negative cash flow may be turned around into a positive cash flow property by re-evaluating and restructuring one or more of the following factors:

- the price of the property
- the amount of the down payment
- the interest rate
- the loan payoff period
- the rents from the property
- the property's operating expenses

Consider how each of these factors can be used.

The price of the property It may be possible to renegotiate a lower price so that the monthly payments are low enough to produce a positive cash flow.

The amount of the down payment Each dollar in the down payment for a property directly reduces the remaining loan balance by one dollar. In effect, by increasing the down payment, and reducing the loan balance, then the future monthly payments will be decreased.

The interest rate Simply stated, the higher the interest rate, the higher the monthly payment. The monthly payment for a $50,000 loan for 30 years at 10% interest is $439. That same loan at 15% interest would require a $632 payment. The 5% change in interest rates results in almost $200 difference in monthly payments.

The loan payoff period A shorter loan-payoff period logically will require higher payments than a long loan-payoff period. For example, a $50,000 loan for 30 years at 13% interest requires a $533 monthly payment. That same loan for 12 years would require a $687 monthly payment, a difference of $134. Of course, by making the higher payments for a shorter period, the property will be paid off sooner, but a negative cash flow may be a more important short-term consideration to the investor than a high equity position in the property.

Property rents It is possible to convert a rental property with negative cash flows to one with positive cash flows simply by raising the rents. This may be done in more than one way. First, it may be possible to raise the rents with no improvements or additional work on the building at all. If the previous rents were well below market, then the tenants will likely be unable to find a comparable residence for less than the new rents, assuming that the new rents do not exceed the market rate. Another strategy is to raise the rents, but at the same time to make improvements in the property. The rents must be increased enough to cover the negative cash flows including any additional expenditures on improvements.

One investor has a standard policy of giving tenants a 30-day notice of increases in their rents within the first month after he purchases a new property. During the following 30 days, without having promised the tenants, he systematically paints, trims, repairs, and generally improves the appearance and quality of the property. He says that few tenants move out and most seem happy with the arrangement. By not promising specific improvements, he can do what he wants and feels he can afford in the 30-day period. Otherwise, the tenants might make certain demands he is unwilling to meet.

He bought one property with contract payments of $403 per month, but which was collecting only $285 in rents a month. That resulted in $188 a month negative cash flow before expenses. By incorporating his system to raise the rents, he was able to collect $605 a month in rents. The additional rents provided a positive cash flow after all expenditures and additional costs of improvements.

Of course, another alternative strategy would be to contract with tenants to raise rents contingent upon specific improvements. Many investors successfully do this.

Property's operating expenditures Property operating expenditures include such things as taxes, insurance, repairs, maintenance, utilities, and management. Taxes and insurance are examples of fixed costs over which the owner has little or no direct control. Other costs, however, are different. The owner can control them at least to some extent. For example, it may appear that garbage costs would be fixed, but it is common for the monthly charge for garbage pick-up to be based upon the number of bins and frequency of service. By decreasing the number of bins, and educating tenants to compact garbage as much as possible, the costs can be reduced significantly.

Some costs, such as maintenance and repairs, may appear to be highly controllable. The rule here is to be prudent. While you as the investor do have control over the timing of these costs, you must pay them in one of three ways:

1. on a regular basis in the form of general upkeep
2. periodically in large amounts as the property falls into major disrepair
3. at the time of sale in the form of a lower sale price.

The amount of the costs to the investor increases the longer these costs are postponed.

Of course, more than one of the above factors may be employed simultaneously to achieve a positive cash flow. The main point is that negative cash flows can be dangerous to an investor's financial health. Before buying any income property, be sure to analyze the cash flows carefully and determine your ability to withstand any apparent negative flows. If you are selling a property on contract, be sure to analyze the future cash flows for the buyer and determine the risks to you associated with any of his negative cash flows. Many Realtors® often ask prospective buyers if they can withstand negative cash flows. You should ask yourself as a seller if *you can afford the risks of selling a property on contract which will produce a negative cash flow for the buyer.*

Too many investors employ an abbreviated analysis of cash flows. This analysis utilizes the following income statement:

Gross income	$____
Less expenses:	
Taxes	$____
Insurance	$____
Water and sewer	$____
Total expenses	$____
Net operating income	$____

This income statement has been dubbed the "seller's income statement." It is called a seller's income statement because it presents an income property in the most favorable light to the buyer, accounting only for certain fixed expenses. To say the least, this income statement is very deceiving. Both the seller and the buyer can be misled. The buyer, because he may be persuaded to buy a property with a negative cash flow when he cannot afford it. The seller, because the success of the contract sale depends upon the buyer's ability to pay for the property. An unexpected negative cash flow for the buyer also puts the seller in jeopardy, as we have illustrated before.

Traditionally, buyers formulate property income statements. On the other hand, the attitude of sellers has been akin to the idea, "Buyer beware." Sellers have seldom produced income and cash flow statements that represent the new buyer's position.

Since contract sales have become so prevalent, and since the fortunes of the buyer and seller are so interrelated, it behooves the seller and the buyer to construct an honest appraisal of a property's income potential. In fact, it would be wise for the seller to produce an income statement reflecting the buyer's cash flow from the property before the sale in order to protect his own interests. By performing this analysis and finding that the new buyer will have a negative cash flow, the seller may decide not to go through with the sale simply because of the risk he would face in the event the buyer cannot afford the property.

The National Association of Realtors has produced a

more accurate operating statement than the one above to tabulate the cash flows generated by a property. A similar, but simpler one (see below), offers the more realistic analysis of positive and negative cash flows.

Name_____
Location_____
Type of property_____

Gross scheduled income .... $_____
Less vacancy .... $_____

Gross operating income .... _____
    Less: Operating expenses
        Taxes .... $_____
        Insurance .... _____
        Management .... _____
        Legal .... _____
        Maintenance and repairs .... _____
        Advertising .... _____
        Sewer and water .... _____
        Rubbish collection .... _____
        Total operating expenses .... $_____

Net operating income .... $_____
Less total monthly debt service .... _____
Cash flow .... $_____

We prefer to construct the statement on a monthly basis because every item except taxes and insurance is either received or paid monthly. Not only are we concerned with net operating income, but also with the actual cash flow. This cash flow determines whether the property can pay for itself without resale or other injections of cash. The yearly statement is used to determine the value of a property and its rate of return.

The seller is in an excellent position to formulate this cash flow statement from the perspective of the buyer, since the seller has had experience of operating the property. If you are buying a piece of rental property and the seller has not provided an income statement (which very likely will be the case), then you should do it yourself. There is nothing wrong with asking the seller to help you with the estimates for the different items on the statement. You may even persuade the seller to review his or her own records on the property with you. If not, be careful with your estimates and check the figures with local authorities.

The different items on the statement should be relatively self-explanatory, except perhaps the estimate of the "vacancy and credit losses." Another term for this item is the "vacancy factor."

It is nearly impossible to operate rental properties with no vacancies at all. The vacancy factor is a percentage of total possible income that will not be earned in a given month or year due to vacancies. The dollar amount of the vacancy factor is computed by multiplying the total possible gross income by the percentage vacancy factor. For example, if a property has a total possible gross income of $1,200 per month and a percentage vacancy factor of 4%, the dollar vacancy factor is $48. This is an estimate and must be calculated in the analysis even if no vacancies have occurred in some months. Other months will experience greater vacancies. The easiest way to find out the yearly percentage vacancy factor in your city is to telephone your local apartment association or rental agencies. You can compute your own figure by determining how many days during the past year your apartments have been vacant, and then dividing that number by 365 times the number of units. For example, suppose each apartment in an eight-unit complex averages being vacant 14 days during the year, the percentage vacancy factor would be computed as follows:

$$\text{Total unit days vacant} = \frac{14 \text{ days} \times 8 \text{ units}}{365 \times 8} = \frac{}{2920} = .0383 \text{ or about } 4\%$$

Sometimes sellers insist that they have no vacancies. This is seldom, if ever, true. When it does happen, it probably means that the rents are much too low. Some sellers also say that when a vacancy occurs it only takes a day or two to fill the vacant unit. Again, this is seldom true. By the time a newly vacated unit is cleaned, advertised, seen by prospective tenants, and a decision is made, at least a week has lapsed. A vacancy factor less than 3% is unrealistic, except perhaps in very rare circumstances.

Another point you should study carefully in the cash-flow evaluation is the percentage of total operating expenses to the total gross income. The total operating expenses probably will be somewhere between 25% and 50% of the total gross income, depending upon the age and condition of the building and also upon who is responsible for such expenses as utilities. If you compute less than 25%, you probably had better do it again to be sure your estimates are reasonable and accurate. The major expenses such as taxes, management, maintenance, and vacancy factor can be expected to run between 5% and 10% each. A combined percentage of 40% is not unreasonable.

You will notice from the following analysis how ridiculous it is for a prospective buyer simply to subtract a mortgage payment from a property's gross income to determine the cash flow. In a recent advertisement it was noticed that a seller was doing exactly what we are warning you about. He was confusing his cash flow before expenses with his cash flow after expenses. His newspaper ad gave the following details:

$440 gross monthly income
$267 monthly payments

$173 positive cash flow

We have yet to see a property operate without incurring expenses. The owner must subtract some 25–50% of his gross monthly income from what is received to estimate his actual cash flow.

No money down

Probably the most talked-about principle in real estate investment during the past five years has been the principle of buying property with no money down. At least two writers have made fortunes from books touting this principle. The most widely used form to buy property with no money down is to use contracts. In some cases, other forms of consideration are given instead of a cash down payment. We presently encounter more than a dozen residential properties a month offered for no money down. To date, we have purchased not one of those properties. If no money down is so attractive, and since we use creative financing techniques, why haven't we purchased properties with no money down? Basically there are two reasons.

7

1. price vs. value—Properties offered with no money down almost invariably are over-priced.
2. negative cash flow—The income from such properties seldom is enough to counter the effect of financing the total purchase price.

We recently attended a seminar on creative financing. The point of the whole seminar was to persuade the people to invest in real estate and to persuade them that it is easy to get rich in real estate. Here is an example of the advice given there.

To illustrate the idea, suppose that we find a four-plex priced at $130,000. The seller is asking a sizable down payment, but we offer to pay $10,000 more for the property if the seller will allow us to purchase it with no down payment. That would make the total purchase price $140,000. The

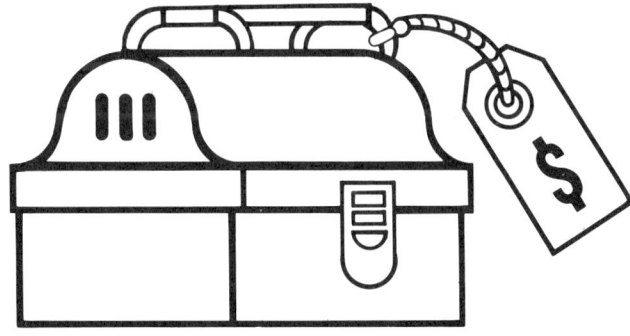

No such thing as a free lunch

leader also suggested that the higher price could persuade the seller to lower the interest on the contract. The argument would go something like this. The higher price gives the seller a capital gain that is taxed at a lower rate than interest income. This is, of course, true since interest is ordinary income and the $10,000 would be capital gains.

As we said, one of the primary problems with property bought with no money down is the very high likelihood of negative cash flows. In order to overcome this problem, the seminar leader asked us to persuade the seller to accept as the monthly payment the total rent collected from the property, less any expenses. Any deficiencies arising from the differences between the normal amortization of the loan and the arranged payments simply would be added to the unpaid loan balance.

Now let's examine this property. In the city where this proposal was made, the units of a four-plex in the $130,000 price range probably would rent for about $275 per month. Monthly income from the proeprty, then, would amount to $1,100. Interest on the $140,000 contract, at 12%, would be $1,400 for the first month. Expenses on the property can be estimated conservatively at 35% of gross scheduled income, or $385 per month. If we subtract these expenses from the gross scheduled income, $715 would be left to apply to the loan—$685 short of the interest alone in the first month. This $685 would be added to the unpaid balance, now leaving us, the buyer, with a new loan balance of $140,685 after one month. If we followed this same procedure for a year, by the end of 12 months, our loan balance would have swollen to $148,687.51. If we sold the property in one year, it would have had to appreciate at a rate of more than 14% just to break even. Remember that the value of the building was $130,000, not $140,000, which was artificially arranged for financing purposes. The value of the building appreciates from $130,000 not $140,000. In today's economy, it is difficult for the market to sustain a 14% growth factor, although there are a few exceptional areas. The leader also suggested that we consider the pessimistic viewpoint. What if the value of the property did not go up at all? What could we as buyers lose, he asked, if we simply walked away from the property? After all, we had paid nothing for it and made no monthly payments. Nothing to lose. At the end of the year it is worth $130,000, but we, as the buyer, will owe $148,687. Although it is possible to walk away from the building, it is not possible to walk away from the $148,687.51 debt. If we walk away from the property, the seller may force its sale to pay the debt we owe. In that case, probably little more than $100,000 will be collected from such a forced sale, leaving a remainder of more than $40,000 debt for which we as the buyer will be liable. That could be more than a small problem. Even if the property sells for its $130,000 value, the remaining debt would amount to more than $18,687. Plus, the litigation costs would be significant, as well as the costs in reputation.

In summary, such an investment described above would have to be based solely upon the premise that property values always increase at a significant rate. This premise simply isn't true. During recent years in many parts of the country property values actually have gone down. It also is questionable to assume that a seller would agree to such an arrangement that would postpone the receipt of such a large amount of the contracted price.

Notice that the primary problem in the example, as is the primary problem on any no-money-down purchase, is *negative cash flow*. A second problem for the seller results from the buyer's lack of equity in the property. In order to follow the seminar leader's advice outlined above, the buyer must place enormous faith in the prospect of property appreciation. In order to make it work, the property must be held for an extended period in an economy experiencing sustained growth. And you must find a willing seller. A well-informed seller would not get entrapped in an arrangement like that one. Also, this combination of factors will discourage a well-informed, conservative investor from actually purchasing a no-money-down "bargain."

Advantages and disadvantages

Buyer

If a buyer can find the right property, for the right price, with a positive cash flow, in favorable economic conditions, a no-money-down deal can be fantastic. The major advantage is that the purchase can be made without any cash. That is a very attractive prospect. Fulfilling these conditions, however, is unlikely, at best. The same investment counselor recently advised several clients to buy any property that even comes close to a positive cash flow, if it were offered for no money down. He admitted that those properties are very rare. The interesting thing about this admission is that it came from a very aggressive investor, whose advice often is based upon unsound speculation rather than informed investment principles.

Seller

Despite any arguments to the contrary, the risks are so great that we know of no good reasons for a seller to offer a property with no down payment. There may be some very untypical sellers who are forced to sell with no down payment, but if given a choice, the seller always should require a reasonable down payment.

The risks to the seller arise from two factors:

1. the risk of negative cash flows to the buyer increases the risk to the seller, as we pointed out before.
2. the buyer often is acquiring little or no equity in a no-money-down financing arrangement. This factor greatly increases the risk of default on the contract.

How to avoid the problem

The buyer and seller can avoid the problems associated with no-money-down financing arrangements by applying the same principles we discussed in the section on negative cash flows. This is true, because as we said, the primary risk in a no-money-down purchase is the probability of negative cash flows. We anticipate, however, that few no-money-down sales will be consummated if these principles are applied.

Borrowing for a down payment

In a no-money-down purchase the seller does not receive a down payment, but in effect finances what would have been a down payment along with the rest of the purchase price. The buyer may, however, borrow a down payment from someone other than the seller. In this case, the seller receives a down payment, which is different from a true no-money-down purchase. Also, the amount borrowed for the down payment typically must be paid back in a much shorter period than the balance of the purchase price. For example, one investor borrowed $10,000 for a down payment on a $66,000 property with a 30-year mortgage. The $10,000 was due in three years. As with the no-money-down purchase, the buyer is able to acquire a property without any personal cash outlay. But also as with the no-money-down purchase, the total purchase price must be paid in the future, and this gives rise to

8

exactly the same problems as with the no-money-down transaction—a high probability of negative cash flows. Only it can be worse, because of the short-term nature of the borrowed down payment. For the first few years the payments for the contract plus the payments on the amount borrowed for the down payment probably will be larger than if the total purchase price had been financed for a full 30 years.

For example, if the investor above had financed the total purchase price of the property at 10½%, the monthly payments would have been $603. By financing the $10,000 down payment at 8% for three years and the remainder at 10¼% for 30 years, the total monthly payments for the first 36 months were $825 excluding taxes and insurance ($313 for the repayment of the down payment plus $512 for the 30-year note). It would be almost impossible for this property to generate a positive cash flow.

Nothing down, nothing left

Some investment counselors are advocating much more creative-financing arrangements for buyers. Here is a typical example. One real estate investment counselor recently retold a story where a buyer borrowed from several sources and even bought merchandise on credit to give to the seller as a down payment. We have changed some of the specific facts of the case in the interest of propriety, but the information is the same.

John found an apartment building with 10 units at a sales price of $200,000. The seller was asking $25,000 down payment and was willing to carry the remainder in a contract over 30 years. John did not have the $25,000 in cash but figured he could still buy the building if he were creative enough.

John knew that by planning the closing date appropriately, he could use money from the first month's rents as part of his down payment. The seller collects all the rent until the building is sold, and the rents are paid in advance. If the rents are paid on the first day of the month and the building is sold on the second, the rents collected by the seller for that month are prorated to the seller for the one day that he owned the building and to the buyer for the rest of the month. The buyer can apply that amount toward the down payment. By using this strategy John was able to reduce the cash needed for the down payment by $1,933. (Total rents for the month were $2,000, i.e., $200 rent per unit, times 10 units. Proration for one day is $67 for the seller. John received the rest.) The security deposits that had been given to the seller when the tenants moved into the property were transferred to John, who applied them to the down payment, although they still belong to the tenant. These amounted to $1,000 (or $100 for each of the 10 apartments). In some states this may be illegal, and the deposits must be held separately in an escrow account for the tenants. The total then required by John for the down payment was $22,067.

Using the creative methods he was taught, John had to find out what the seller would use the $22,067 for. First he learned that the seller was required to pay a commission to the real estate agent of 6% of the sales price, or $12,000. John negotiated with the agent to take a note from him for the full $12,000 at 15% interest, due in three years, rather than collect it immediately from the seller. The balance remaining for the down payment had been diminished to $10,067.

John found out that the seller intended to buy a new car with the money collected from the down payment. He convinced the seller to pick out the car he wanted and let John purchase it. The total cost of the car was $8,000, leaving only $2,067 for John to pay. John, being the creative fellow he was, borrowed this final amount from his mother-in-law. The following tabulation shows the different sources of John's down payment on the property:

Rents	$1,933
Security deposits	1,000
Sales commission	12,000
Automobile	8,000
Personal loan	2,067
Total	$25,000

Let's examine the cash flows of this proposed purchase. If we assume no payments on the $12,000 note and no monthly payments on the $2,067 personal loan, that leaves only monthly payments for the automobile and the balance of the contract. At 15% interest on the $8,000 car for 48 months, the monthly payment would be $222. Payments on the $175,000 balance on the contract would be $1,666, assuming 11% interest for 30 years. Let's consider operating expenses at a conservative 35% of the gross scheduled income. Gross scheduled income was given as $2,000 per month, resulting in operating expenses estimated at about $700 per month. Cash outflow, then, is estimated at $2,576. Only $2,000 (10 × 200) inflow is expected each month, for a negative cash flow of $588 monthly. The following tabulation summarizes this monthly cash flow:

Gross rents received	$2,000
Less:	
Contract payments	−1,666
Auto payments	− 222
Expenses	− 700
Net cash flow	$− 588

Remember that this figure does not consider provisions for the $12,000 note for the sales commission and the $2,067 personal loan from the buyer's mother-in-law. Consider first the effect of the $12,000 note. Of course, this assumes he is able to find a real estate agent who is willing to make such an arrangement, which is unlikely in the first place. Perhaps possible, but unlikely. John has at least two options on meeting this obligation which will amount to $18,767 in three years. John may either set aside some money each month, letting it earn interest in the meantime, so that he will have the $12,000 plus interest of $6,767 at the end of three years. That would require $416 per month, assuming an interest rate of 15% that he can earn on the savings during the three years. If he does this, the $416 represents additional negative cash flow—now almost $1,000 per month. Suppose John did not save monthly, but instead depended upon proceeds from resale of the building to pay this note. He would have to pay this out of the down payment he receives at that time, which could be a problem if the next buyer uses such creative financing techniques as John did.

If John's mother-in-law actually expects repayment of her loan to him, then the $2,067 loan represents additional negative cash flow or a need for more cash upon resale. If she simply gave him the money, then good for John.

The automobile poses an interesting problem for the seller. Notice that the car is not his, plus he is dependent upon John to pay for it. What if John defaults? It will be embarrassing to walk out of church one Sunday morning and find a tow truck taking his car away to be repossessed by the loan company. Remember that any merchandise that a buyer gives a seller as down payment is not the seller's if the buyer purchased it on credit.

Suppose the seller had anticipated not having title to the new car and had the loan put in his name. The seller is still dependent upon John for the payments, and if John doesn't pay, then the seller gets the bad credit rating or is saddled with the monthly payments. The point is, do not accept merchandise from a buyer who still owes on it.

Advantages and disadvantages

Buyer

The previous discussion with the case indicates that the only advantage of borrowing the down payment for the buyer is to be able to purchase a property without any immediate cash outlay. On the other hand, we have illustrated that it is almost impossible (we would say impossible, only there always seems to be an exception to every rule) to buy a property this way and still turn a positive cash flow. A general rule that might be helpful is that if the down payment has to be borrowed, then the buyer probably cannot afford the property.

Seller

Two problems face the seller when a buyer has to borrow a down payment. First, the seller shares the buyer's risk of negative cash flows, as we have discussed at length before. Secondly, when a buyer gives merchandise that is not paid for as a down payment, then the seller does not control ownership of the merchandise and runs a great risk of losing it.

How to avoid the problem

The best advice we can give you as a seller is to be cautious in these kinds of transactions. We fully expect that if you are cautious, you will not sell under these circumstances. Our advice to buyers considering borrowing down payments is the same as we gave for negative cash flows. Don't do it unless you can support financially the negative cash flows, even then there may be surprises.

Subordinations and double closings

Subordination in real estate means that a lender voluntarily takes a lower mortgage priority position on a property than he is otherwise entitled to. This occurs when the lender allows a new, second lender to have priority over his position. For example, a person owns a $15,000 vacant lot free and clear. A buyer wants to purchase the lot and build a home on it. The buyer wants the seller to finance the purchase with an installment contract. This would give the seller first position on the property. The buyer then approaches a bank to borrow money for the building, and attempts to use the land as collateral. Since the seller is in the first position on the land, the bank most likely will be unwilling to take a second position on the property. In order to facilitate the sale, the seller agrees to give the bank first position on the property and take a second position himself. What this means is that

9

if the property goes into foreclosure, the bank will be paid first from the proceeds of the foreclosure sale. The seller will receive payment with whatever is left over, if any. In some states the bank and the seller will receive what are called legal judgments against the borrower for the amount of the deficiencies, but since the borrower probably will not have any money (or he would have paid the loans), there is a slim chance that the deficiencies will be paid, except perhaps in very small increments over a very long time.

The arrangements for a subordination are made when the buyer, the seller, and a representative from the lending institution meet at one time in a single closing. All contracts for the loans on the property are completed at this meeting.

Subordination has been a valuable tool for builders and land developers. It has provided needed funds that could not otherwise be obtained to improve properties.

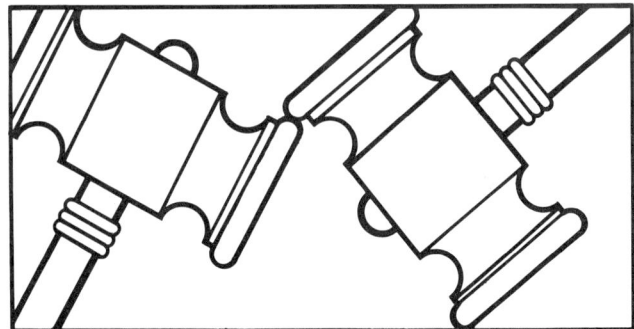

A double whammy

Advocates of creative financing, however, have adopted the principle to new ends, that is, to enable buyers to purchase property with none of their own money down and actually put cash in their pockets for either personal purposes or reinvestment.

The mechanics of subordination in a creative financing arrangement go something like this: first, the seller gives the buyer free and clear title to the property without any payment. The buyer then acquires a first mortgage from a conventional lending institution. The buyer finally will make the down payment to the seller from these loan proceeds, at which time a final contract is drawn between the buyer and seller, establishing the second position of the seller. This represents a second closing on the property. The buyer is free then to use the rest of the money from the conventional loan for other purposes.

Notice the difference between how professional developers arrange subordination and how many buyers use subordination in creative financing. Professional developers make sure that the total transaction is completed at one time in a single closing in order to preserve the integrity of the title and to protect the sellers. Some creative buyers, however, require that the seller give them title with the understanding that they, the buyers, will make all the necessary arrangements with the institutional lender. This may even be done out of "consideration" for the seller in order not to "inconvenience" him or her. Between the time of the first closing, when the seller gives title of the property to the buyer, and the second closing, the seller's position is totally unsecured. It was this very arrangement that led to the half-million dollar loss experienced by the woman selling the apartment complex that we discussed in chapter 2.

Advantages and disadvantages

Buyer

Despite what you might hear from other sources, there are no advantages to the buyer and seller using subordinations with double closings for the sole purpose of generating cash for the buyer. The apparent advantages for the buyer are that properties may be purchased totally with other people's money, and extra funds are available for whatever use the buyer sees fit. An example may help to see why this argument is only illusory.

Our example is an exact case given by a well-known real estate counselor. We have changed the numbers to reflect a realistic market, but the loan-to-value ratios are exactly the same as in the original case.

Suppose a buyer purchases a property for $60,000 which is its exact value in the market. The seller agrees to take $12,000 down and carry a contract for $48,000 in a second position. After receiving title, but before making a down payment, the buyer secured a first mortgage from an institutional lender for $44,000. The buyer paid $12,000 from the proceeds of the loan as down payment on the property and pocketed the remaining $32,000. At this point the buyer owed $92,000 on the $60,000 property.

Sales price	$60,000
Down payment	−12,000
Financed with seller	$48,000
Financed with seller	$48,000
Loan from bank	+44,000
Total loans on property	$92,000

Payments on the total debt were estimated at $972.56 ($471.32 on the first mortgage and $501.24 on the second lien). There is almost no way that the property could generate a positive cash flow. Rents were estimated at $800. Taxes and insurance were estimated to be about $100 per month. The negative cash flow totalled $272.56 plus the effects of repairs, utilities, management, and so on.

The advisor also pointed out two benefits to this purchase over and above the $32,000 already in the pocket of the buyer:

1. the equity build up of the property and

2. the increased value of the property through appreciation.

There is no equity by definition until the value of the asset owned is greater than the total amount of the loans against the property. Assuming 10% inflation on the property, it would take between four and five years for this to occur.

In the early years, appreciation will only serve to increase the value of the property up to the amount of the loans against it. In the meantime, the buyer faces a heavy monthly negative cash flow.

Perhaps the strangest phenomenon about this kind of transaction is the illusion of gaining net worth by pocketing the additional cash. This cash does not increase net worth at all. You may be getting the $32,000 in cash, but you still owe it to the lender. If you spend it, you still owe it.

You must remember that the only way for this strategy to pay off for the buyer is for him to hold the property for many years in a strong real estate market and use the extra money generated from the original loan to support the negative cash flows. Even then, the tactic is very risky. We don't do it and we don't advise it to others.

Seller

While double closings may seem advantageous to the buyer in very extreme circumstances (and only then), there is no advantage whatsoever for the seller. By giving away title to a property with no compensation from the buyer, the seller has done just that, given it away. Even if the total process were covered in the offer to purchase agreement, the buyer's debt is unsecured against the property until the second closing. Should the buyer choose not to show up for the second closing, the seller's only recourse is to sue for damages. If the buyer had successfully acquired a large sum of funds from the lender by using the property as collateral, it may be difficult even to find him. The bank is the only party with any legal interest in the property other than the buyer. The seller has given it away. Typically, the lender does not want the property, but the money. If the seller is lucky, he may persuade the lender to let him take back the property and assume the mortgage. But then he is saddled with the large debt contracted by the buyer, who has the money.

Suppose that everything goes fine. The buyer follows through, makes the down payment and signs the final contract. The seller still is in a risky second position. If the buyer defaults to the bank on the payments, the property would be sold at auction to satisfy the debt owed the bank. The purchase price paid at the auction would be somewhere between $44,000, the amount owed, and $60,000, the fair market value. Probably, the auction price would be in the neighborhood of the lesser amount. If the foreclosure sale were to net the full market value of $60,000, which almost never occurs, the most the seller would net would be $16,000, leaving a net loss of $32,000—the amount that the buyer put into his pocket.

How to avoid the problem

Do not buy or sell using double closing in creative financing arrangements unless the buyer is willing to secure the debt to the seller with another valuable piece of property, giving the seller first position on the other property. You are not likely to get it, so forget it.

Handyman specials

A common bit of advice given to new real estate investors is to buy the worst home in a neighborhood, fix it up, and then sell it at a substantial profit. The term "handyman special" implies that the buyer will fix it up and charge the new buyer for the time and energy spent to do the work. Recent years have witnessed a surge in these properties as investments.

Advantages and disadvantages

Buyer

You should know right now that property that requires more than a coat of paint, some new carpet, and handy work you

10

can do yourself is a dangerous investment. Certainly, handyman specials can be quite profitable for the right investor—that is, the one with a lot of experience in carpentry, plumbing, and like skills. If you must hire the skilled craftsman, however, the handyman special is not a wise investment. Remember, if you do it yourself, it will look like you did it yourself. If you are a professional, it will be a professional job. But if not, you may hurt its resale value.

Even when you do have the skills necessary to fix up a property, you must be careful, because too often handyman specials are overpriced. We recently saw a duplex offered as a handyman special for $65,000. After estimating the total cost of repairs, the final cost of the property was conservatively estimated at about $110,000. We estimated the value of the property, using an income method, at between $90,000 and $100,000 after the fix up.

Buy low, sell low

You also need to understand that if you deal in this kind of property, you need a significant amount of cash. In the properties that you are likely to find, you will need at least a small down payment, and a large amount of cash for the planned repairs. The reason you need to have the cash for repairs up front is because it is difficult to get large loans on dilapidated property. You might be able to charge some materials and a few tools, but when you begin needing a new roof, furnaces, complete bathrooms, stairways, and kitchens, that will require many thousands of dollars. Typically, this kind of fix-up requires cash. It becomes especially acute when the property has been condemned.

In 1981 we saw a property advertised and sold as a handyman special for about $37,500. The property had been condemned and was in very dilapidated condition. To make the offer more attractive, payments on the property were not to begin for six months after the sale. The buyer evidently figured he could buy it, complete the fix-up before the six-month period ended, and then sell the property or rent it at a substantial profit. A year later, the property appears to be less than half finished and is on the market again as a "ran out of money sale." The buyer now is faced with trying to sell an old, half-fixed up property at a price that is almost certain to result in substantial losses.

Seller

The advantages to the seller of a fix-up property are straightforward:

1. The seller has sold a property without going to the expense of repairing it himself.
2. By calling the property a "handyman special," the seller sometimes can make more profit by leaving the property in a dilapidated condition than by fixing it and selling it at a higher price. Although the price is lower, the markup is higher.

Handyman specials actually seem to have a kind of value of their own in today's market among certain buyers.

The disadvantage to the seller is that when selling to an uninformed and unprepared buyer, the danger of the buyer running out of money and quitting the contract is very high. What appeared a certain sale in the beginning will have turned into a repossession, foreclosure, possible law suit, and a renewed effort to sell the property, which now has half-finished repairs that may not suit the taste of any new potential buyers.

How to avoid the problem

The best advice we have is for you to leave these handyman specials to professionals who have enough money to renovate a building correctly and sell it at a profit. You may be able to pull it off, but remember that many cannot.

If you are the seller, it will pay you to determine the buyer's qualifications to follow through on the contract and successfully fix up and sell the property. You can be sure that if an institution were lending the money that it would seek such assurance. Since you are financing the property on contract, you will want the same assurances.

"Due on sale" clauses

A "due on sale" clause is a form of acceleration clause. In general, acceleration clauses in contracts state that upon the occurrence of certain events, the lender has the right to demand payment of the total unpaid loan balance. The "due on sale" clause specifies that upon the resale of the property, the full balance of a property loan may be demanded. For example, suppose Mary buys a property from Warren on contract; and the contract provides that if Mary resells the property before final payment has been made, Warren can call due the full unpaid balance at the time of resale.

11

Advantages and disadvantages

Buyer

Buyers tend to view due on sale clauses as a disadvantage because they give the buyers less flexibility in financing any resale of the property.

The major problem with these clauses is that buyers sometimes are not aware of them in the contract, or, if they are aware, they sometimes intentionally try to violate them. In either case, a property may be resold by the buyer without paying the balance due, and then the seller (or lender) demands payment or forecloses the property.

In a recent case, a seller tried to sell a house on contract with a nominal down payment. The seller, however, was paying on a mortgage with a due on sale clause and did not

Pay the piper

have enough money to pay off the loan. The seller tried to convince one would-be buyer that the due on sale clause in the mortgage contract was unenforceable.

If a new buyer were to purchase the property and were unaware of the due on sale clause in the seller's contract with the mortgage holder, then the buyer could be in for an unfortunate surprise when the previous lender found out about the sale through researching the titles. If the seller is unable to make full payment as required, the mortgage holder may then be able to repossess the property with no compensation whatever to the new buyer.

You need to remember that acceleration clauses may be included in both conventional mortgages and owner-financing contracts.

Seller

Due on sale clauses are an advantage primarily to the seller. They may be used effectively for two purposes:

1. They can prevent the seller from becoming involved in a contract chain, which we already have stated can be a problem for both buyers and sellers.
2. Due on sale clauses also can be an effective method to renegotiate interest rates on long-term loans.

When a property is resold by the buyer, the seller can demand the total unpaid balance, or renegotiate a new loan at a new interest rate. Due on sale clauses, then, become strategic advantages for the seller. They give the seller more control.

How to avoid the problem

Buyers need to research all documents previously signed by the seller with other lenders to determine the presence of any due on sale clauses. Secondly, if there is such a clause, the buyer must be assured that the seller has fulfilled these requirements or has a waiver from the previous lender at the time of closing. Sellers, on the other hand, should use a due on sale clause to protect their interest and then follow up periodically to determine whether there have been any resales.

Due on sale clauses are being scrutinized legally in many states. Some states have written new laws limiting the use of due on sale clauses. You should check the laws in your state to determine their applicability and enforceability in financing contracts.

Price vs. value

A major consideration in evaluating a real estate investment is its price versus its value. The *price* of a property is the agreed-upon number of dollars that represents the exchange between the buyer and the seller. We can call this an exchange price, which may or may not correspond to the property's value. How many times have you heard someone say, "Boy, I got a real steal on that property" or, "He really got taken on that deal"? These statements indicate that the prices were significantly different from the values. How is it that these differences occur, and what does it mean to you as a real estate buyer or seller?

Let's examine a standard definition of market value. Here is one given in a college textbook on real estate principles:

12

Market value, also called fair market value, is the highest price in terms of money that a property will bring if (1) the terms are all cash to the seller, (2) the property is exposed on the open market for a reasonable length of time, (3) the buyer and seller are fully informed as to market conditions and the uses to which the property may be put, (4) neither is under abnormal pressure to conclude a transaction, and (5) the seller is capable of conveying marketable title.

Bruce Harwood, *Real Estate Principles*,
Reston Publishing Co., Inc., 1977

Using this definition, we can see how the final sales price may not coincide with the "market value" of a property as defined above. For example, notice that the definition specifies that the market value is the "highest price." This stipulation assumes that every potential buyer is aware of the property and that the seller is aware of the highest price any of those

Mirages on the horizon

buyers is willing to pay. Even though the real estate business community makes considerable efforts to fulfill this ideal condition, it still remains the ideal and often is not achieved. Consequently, the market value may be different from the actual sales price. We could show how failure to fulfill any one of the above conditions could affect the price, effectively changing it from its true market value. But the point should be clear: the price of a property and its value are not necessarily the same amount.

Determination of value

This differentiation between price and value is important to you as a real estate buyer or seller because you must determine if the price of a property is in line with its value. While it may be impossible to determine the single true value of a property, experienced real estate investors use three methods to approximate that value:

1. the income approach,
2. the market method, and
3. replacement cost.

Replacement costs and the market method are appropriate for all buyers and sellers. The income approach, however, may be used only by investors in income properties, such as apartment buildings.

Income approach

The income method computes the value of a property based upon expected future income. These computations range from the very simple to extremely sophisticated mathematical models. A frequently used method is the computation of the capitalization (CAP) rate.

We must warn you, however, that this income approach can be misleading if used inappropriately. It projects income far into the future and makes numerous assumptions about what the future markets and interest rates are going to be. Even the best investors often miss the mark when trying to predict future conditions. We distrust the CAP rate and seldom use it. But you need to understand its computation so that you can be informed when others discuss it.

Capitalization rate An initial assessment of the value of a property may be computed in the following four steps:

Step 1. Determine the expected total annual gross income.

Step 2. Estimate the expected annual expenses to operate the property, such as taxes, insurance, utilities, vacancy, maintenance, repairs, and so forth.

Step 3. Subtract the expenses from the gross income, which gives you the net operating income.

Step 4. Compute the capitalization rate for the property.

$$\text{CAP rate} = \frac{\text{Net Operating Income}}{\text{Price}}$$

The CAP rate usually will run between .05 (5%) and .10 (10%). The higher the CAP rate the better, since that represents a high income to price ratio. If the CAP rate is in the neighborhood of 5%, you probably should avoid that property. If, on the other hand, the CAP rate is 9% or 10%, you should probably consider it further.

If you want to compute a rough estimate of what the building probably should be worth, you can change the calculation like this:

$$\frac{\text{Net Operating Income}}{\text{Desired CAP Rate}} = \text{Estimated Value}$$

To make this calculation, you probably will use either 9% or 10% as your desired CAP rate, although these values may change with general changes in the economy and fluctuations in interest rates.

You probably will find that in many markets a CAP rate of 10% is almost impossible to find. We are finding fewer of these properties than ever before, although there still are some in the market where we invest. There are at least two reasons so few of these properties seem to be available. First, is the *bigger fool theory*. The bigger fool theory simply states that an investor buys a property at what might already be an inflated price and then tries to find a bigger fool to sell it to. Secondly, investors now place predominant importance upon property appreciation. The advent of so many new investors in the market who are willing to forego short-term income from rents for expected long-term income from appreciation in property values has forced up the prices of many properties, while rents have not kept the same pace. This kind of investment is very risky and highly speculative. The amount to be made from this kind of investment has diminished considerably in recent years, since the sellers themselves have anticipated the buyer's strategy and have based the prices of properties upon anticipated inflation and ignored current income being generated from the properties. It is hard to predict where these trends are leading the market, but for now, the above general guidelines for a desirable CAP rate still seem to be the most appropriate for this method.

The only appropriate use of a simple income approach is to make a first rough assessment of an income property's value. This assessment can be done in two ways. The first computes the CAP rate and compares it to a standard rate. The second actually computes an estimated value of the property.

Gross rent multipliers Technically, gross rent multipliers are not an income approach, because expenses have not been subtracted from the revenues. However, the multipliers are directly related to income generated from properties, assuming a constant percentage of expenses for all properties. The figure is even rougher than the CAP rate computation. The multiplier for a property using this method is determined as follows:

$$\frac{\text{Price}}{\text{Annual Gross Rents}} = \text{Gross Rent Multiplier}$$

As a general rule, the lower the multiplier the better. Current multipliers are running in the neighborhood of 10, which not long ago was considered to be unreasonably high. This trend would indicate again that property prices are not being pegged to income, but rather to expected future appreciation. Consequently, the ultimate result will be that you will have harder times finding properties with positive cash flows. There are indications that in some parts of the country this trend may soon turn around, but for now be patient and shop very carefully.

These two methods of assessing the values of property are best used to compare a prospective property with others in the market. They do not necessarily give you precise measures of the true market values. They must be used with great caution and must be interpreted only as ballpark figures. If you want to be more precise in computing the values of properties using the income approach, you will have to become familiar with more sophisticated techniques. These may be referenced in more technical texts on real estate financing like the *Real Estate Appraiser's Kit* (Barbara S. Miller, Institute For Business Planning, Englewood Cliffs, N.J., 1981). The authors use both the simple approaches shown here and the more sophisticated techniques. The simple models offer initial comparisons of properties, and the more complete income analysis is a great help in calculating a more specific value. We must admit, however, that many successful investors do not use anything other than the ones shown here.

Market method

This method compares properties in the area that are similar to the property in which you are interested and that have recently been sold. Since few properties are identical, it is necessary to make adjustments for significant differences in the properties that might help account for differences in their prices. The condition of repair, number of rooms, sizes of lots, location, and so forth, all can make sizable differences in the values of properties.

Replacement cost method

The replacement cost method computes the cost to construct a new building equivalent to the one already on the property. This cost is added to the value of the land to determine the total replacement value of the property. The land value is usually determined by the market value approach. The replacement cost for the building is determined in one of three ways:

1. A quantity survey may be taken to compute all of the costs for all of the necessary materials and labor. For example, count the number of bricks say, 1,594 and then multiply this by their unit cost of 17 cents—1,594 × .17 = $270.98 is the cost of the bricks. Then do this for each single item in the building. This is the most accurate method, but also the most time consuming.
2. Building components in place, such as fireplaces or an installed roof, may be priced individually and summed to compute the total estimate. This is generally considered the second most accurate method.
3. An estimate also can be made more simply by determining the size of the building either in cubic

feet or square feet, and then multiplying the size by a standard cost per unit foot. For example, a building may have 4,000 square feet. Assuming building costs of $35.00 per square foot, the total estimated replacement cost is $140,000.00. While this third method is generally considered the least accurate, it is by far the most frequently used. This is because the differences among the three often are not large enough to warrant the additional time required to gather all of the necessary information and make the additional computations. When comparing cost on a per foot basis be sure all comparable buildings are of identical construction.

As you practice computing values of properties and as you gain experience in investments, you will improve your ability to assess values. At that point, you will be better able to compensate quickly for imperfections in the calculation methods.

We must caution you again that if you want to use the income approach seriously for anything other than very general comparisons, you will need to study more advanced techniques than we have illustrated here.

Comparison of price vs. value

Once you have estimated the value of a property, then you will compare that value to the price asked by the seller. If you determine that the price is below the estimated value, then you probably will buy it. If you determine that the price is above the value, then you probably will not. This procedure is simple enough, or so it would seem. What happens, however, when a seller offers a property at more than one price, depending upon financing arrangements: What price do you compare to the estimated value?

We have seen properties advertised at one price for cash at the date of sale or another price if financed over future years. For example, it is not unusual to see an advertisement in the real estate section of the classified ads similar to the following:

> IN A HURRY—4 bedroom rambler, garage, workshop, two fireplaces, fenced yard, great view. $90,000, seller carries a contract, or 20 percent discount for cash.

In this case, the price written in the sales contract would read either $90,000 (if financed) or $72,000 (for cash). What price do you compare to what you have determined to be the value of the property? If you have estimated the value to be $80,000, then $90,000 doesn't look so good, but $72,000 looks much better.

You must remember that regardless of how a transaction is presented to you, *there is only one value for a property.* That value is the amount of cash a seller is willing to accept at the date of sale in full exchange for the property. In the above case, that value is $72,000. The $18,000 difference represents interest being charged by the seller if he or she finances it for the buyer. What this $18,000 does is to reduce the interest rate written into the contract, but it is interest just the same. In some cases the difference between the cash sale and an installment sale will be held to be interest, and subject to the laws concerning usury.

A second point needs to be made with regard to price vs. value. We recently attended a real estate seminar offered by a well-known investor advocating no-money-down purchases. In one example the seminar leader suggested that a beginning investor offer the seller $10,000 more than the asking price if the seller would accept an offer for no money down. Ask yourself, is the new price (including the additional $10,000) the value of the property? No. Remember *that the property appreciation will begin at the property's value at the time of sale, not necessarily at the sales price.* What happens then, if you want to sell it shortly afterward? You probably will be forced to take a significant loss on the property unless you can find a bigger fool. The emphasis in creative financing on the terms of purchases has overshadowed the importance of comparing the value and price of a property. Any smart buyer or seller will not ignore this important consideration.

Forfeiture and foreclosure

Forfeiture and foreclosure are ominous terms, ringing of distress and ill luck. There almost always is the good guy-bad guy connotation. In a way, they have been the unmentionables of the real estate business. People don't like to talk about them. They represent failure, and failure is a no-no topic in many current circles promoting real estate investment.

Both forfeiture and foreclosure, however, are very much a part of the real world environment of real estate. In order to successfully buy and sell property, you need to understand both, because in both cases, the financial stakes are enormous. By misunderstanding either one, or both, you can lose far more than your shirt. First we discuss forfeiture, and then foreclosure.

13

Forfeiture

According to the *Real Estate License Examination Study Manual* published by the State of California Department of Real Estate (Sacramento, California), *forfeiture* is defined as the "loss of money or anything of value due to failure to perform." This means that if the buyer fails to fulfill the requirements of the contract, he may be forced to forfeit his rights to the property and any previous payments given to the seller. A typical uniform sales contract might read something like this one from the state of Utah, relating to forfeiture:

> Seller shall have the right, upon failure of the Buyer to remedy the default within five days after written notice, to be released from all obligations to law and in equity to convey said property, and *all payments which have been*

Float like a butterfly, sting like a bee

> *made* theretofore on this contract by the Buyer, *shall be forfeited to the Seller as liquidated damages* for the nonperformance of the contract, and *the Buyer agrees that the Seller may at his option re-enter and take possession of said premises.* [Italics added.]

The italicized portion of this statement indicates that the buyer forfeits all rights to the property, including any and all previous payments made on the property. The fact that both the buyer and the seller sign the agreement containing a statement similar to the one above would ordinarily be assumed to bind both parties to this agreement. This provision tends to give sellers a sense of security that if anything goes wrong, they may repossess the property and retain all previous considerations paid by the buyer. Theirs too often may be a false sense of security.

This false security can be illustrated with a landmark court case in the State of Utah. In *Perkin vs. Spencer* (121 Utah 468, 243 P.2d 446 [1952]), the court ruled that the total of all previous payments on a property by the buyer were "unreasonable and exhorbitant" damages and served to "shock the conscience" of the court. The seller was awarded damages for the buyer's breach of contract, but the damages were determined to be much less than the total payments that had been made. This case has been used as precedent for many other such cases in the State of Utah. Similar cases may exist in other states.

So, there are circumstances when the forfeiture provisions of the contract will not provide a windfall profit to the seller, regardless of any agreement made by the buyer and the seller.

Foreclosure

The definition for "foreclosure" given in the *Real Estate License Examination Study Manual* is:

Procedure whereby property pledged as security for a debt is sold to pay the debt in event of default in payments or terms.

When the buyer fails to make payments as contracted on the loan, the seller has the option to have the property sold in accordance with the laws of the state and to receive the proceeds as payment on the loan. If the proceeds are less than the balance owed by the buyer then the buyer may or may not be liable for the difference, depending upon the applicable state laws. After the sale of the property in the foreclosure process, the buyer may have a *period of redemption*, during which time he can repurchase the property for cash at its foreclosure sale price plus additional charges for the redemption itself. The buyer has no further rights to the property if he has not exercised his rights during the redemption period.

In Utah, as an example, the *Uniform Real Estate Contract* paragraph dealing with foreclosure reads as follows:

> The Seller shall have the right, as his option, and upon written notice to the Buyer, to declare the entire unpaid balance hereunder at once due and payable, and may elect to treat this contract as a note and mortgage, and pass title to the Buyer subject hereto, and proceed immediately for foreclosure the same in accordance with the laws of the State of Utah, and have the property sold and the proceeds applied to the payment of the balance owing, including costs and attorney's fees; and the Seller may have a judgment for any deficiency which may remain. In the case of foreclosure, the Seller hereunder, upon the filing of a complaint, shall be immediately entitled to the appointment of a receiver to take possession of said mortgaged property and collect the rents, issues, and profits therefrom and apply the same to the payment of the obligations hereunder, or hold the same pursuant to order of the court; and the Seller, *upon entry of judgment of foreclosure, shall be entitled to the possession of the said premises during the period of redemption.* [Italics added.]

The italicized portion of the above statement indicates that the seller may remove the buyer from the property in the process of foreclosure during the period of redemption.

On the other hand, this provision often is unenforceable. In Utah, for example, where the above condition is contained in the uniform sales contract, the laws and courts have upheld the buyer's right in many cases to remain on the property during the six-month period of redemption, often rent free (*Local Realty Co. vs. Lindquist*, 96 Utah 297, 85 P.2d 770 [1938]).

Problems of forfeiture and foreclosure

Our examples of contracts providing for forfeiture and foreclosure both come from Utah, and exact provisions in your state may be somewhat different. But the point is the same. Both of these provisions can be deceptive, as others may be where you live. We reiterate our previous advice to consult with competent professional counsel when entering any real estate contract.

Forfeitures and foreclosures can be very complicated and represent significant danger to the real estate investor, as the following example shows.

An investor sold a small apartment complex, requiring a $27,000 down payment from the buyer and a monthly payment of about $2,500. Several months later, the buyer defaulted. The investor then looked to the contract to see what remedies were available to him. The contract contained

1. a forfeiture clause
2. a provision allowing him to sue the buyer for recovery and damages
3. a foreclosure clause.

He first considered forfeiture. When consulting with his attorney, however, the following factors became apparent.

Even though the contract stated explicitly that the investor could recover the property and retain all payments made by the buyer as damages, the courts in that state probably would not uphold this provision unless the seller could prove damages of $27,000 plus all other monies the buyer had paid. Most of the monies, including much of the $27,000 down payment, may have to be returned to the buyer before the investor could take back the property. Since the investor already had reinvested the $27,000, that remedy was impossible.

Second, he determined with his attorney that if he sued the buyer for the defaulted payments, he probably would have to go through the same time-consuming procedure to collect most, if not all, future monthly payments, perhaps even one at a time. Consequently, this remedy also proved to be unsatisfactory.

Foreclosure was the final remedy provided by the contract. This procedure would have involved the courts and taken several months, during which time a court-appointed receiver would collect the rents in order to pay all the underlying debts and obligations on the property so that the seller himself would not go into default. Interestingly, while the obligations are being paid by the receiver, the investor is not paid any profits from the proceeds. What is more, in this case, the property had been allowed to deteriorate badly in just a few months, plus it was only two-thirds rented. The proceeds collected from rents by the receiver would not even cover the obligations of the seller against the building. There was a question as to who should be responsible for the difference between what was collected and what was owed, the investor or the buyer. Also, the apartments that were vacant were damaged and unsuitable to rent. The question existed as to who should be responsible to repair those units. Remember, too, that the receiver is only responsible to collect the rents and pay the necessary expenses on the building. Who would manage the property during the suit, before a judgment was made?

Also, the buyers were delinquent on their payment for utility services to the building. If those services were shut off, all the tenants would move, leaving the building vacant with no income whatsoever.

Another question existed regarding the redemption period. If the buyer could successfully retain possession of the property during the redemption period, he possibly could avoid paying rents during that time. Even if the investor had successfully reacquired the property in foreclosure, he would have difficulty reselling it, since the previous buyer (the one who had defaulted) could redeem the property. Any potential new buyer either would avoid this possibility and not buy the building, or would require a significant discount in price to compensate for the risk of losing the property upon redemption.

In this case, the seller was the third member of a contract chain on the property. This complicated the prospect of foreclosure even more.

The point is that all three remedies provided by the contract were unsatisfactory. The investor was forced to settle with the buyer out of court in a complete renegotiation of terms. Since legal remedies provided by the contract were inadequate, the buyer had the advantage in all new bargaining, because he continued collecting rents from the property, while the seller was required to continue making full payments to the previous mortgage holders. This financial strain forced the seller to settle quickly for terms that otherwise might not have been acceptable.

The provisions in the uniform sales contract to protect the seller failed miserably in this case. The seller had very little real protection. Even though the contract stated that the investor could foreclose and collect the rents, issues, and profits to pay the underlying mortgage, there were no profits. In fact, the building was in much worse condition than it had been when it was sold. It was one-third vacant; and services and utilities were about to be stopped because of nonpayment, which would have forced the rest of the tenants out and eliminated all income from the property. Any sense of security the investor felt at the time of sale surely was exterminated at the end.

Better remedies

The two best remedies for problems that can arise in forfeitures and foreclosures are preventive in nature. They are

1. a trust deed
2. a quitclaim deed used in conjunction with the uniform sales contract.

The advantage that a trust deed offers is that foreclosure avoids judicial involvement and can be accomplished quickly. Also, the trustor (the borrower) does not have redemption rights after the foreclosure sale of property. The trust deed would be used instead of a uniform sales contract. A quitclaim deed simply conveys back to the seller any rights that the buyer might have had in the property. The quitclaim deed is executed at the time of sale along with the uniform sales contract. The quitclaim deed, along with a set of instructions, then is put in escrow with a third party, usually a financial institution, who will hold it until the buyer either defaults or completes the contracted payments. If the buyer defaults, the seller can recover the quitclaim deed from the escrow agent and have the deed recorded, at which time the property is returned to the seller. The advantages of a quitclaim deed are similar to those of a trust deed, and also, the quitclaim deed provides an efficient method of transferring ownership back to the seller in the event of forfeiture.

Although these remedies are not perfect in every case, they do offer better protection for sellers than do standardized installment sales contracts.

Qualifying the buyer

Now that you understand some of the important pitfalls of creative financing, let's consider perhaps the most important element of all when selling your property on contract—your buyer. Of all of the things that can go wrong, the one that can wind up costing you the most is dealing with an unqualified or a dishonest buyer. Throughout previous chapters we have described numerous buyers who have taken advantage of sellers using creative financing. Some of these buyers did it knowingly. Invariably, the costs to the sellers were great, and those costs represent a grave injustice. But the sellers must share the blame in most of the cases. Because of their eagerness to sell and their willingness to make a sale as "convenient" and easy for the buyer as possible, they failed to take common precautions that every commercial lender considers fundamental to any loan decision.

14

When a commercial lender considers any loan, the first consideration is the buyer, then the property. The first question asked is, "Can he and will he pay for it?" Short of clairvoyance, this question usually can be answered in a relatively simple three-step process:

1. requiring the borrower to complete a credit form
2. conducting a credit check
3. evaluating the information collected in the first two steps

Certainly, by answering these questions, the seller cannot quarantee payment, but by evaluating the buyer's current financial position and past credit performance, the seller can assess the likelihood of receiving contracted payments.

Some sellers simply feel unable or unwilling to go

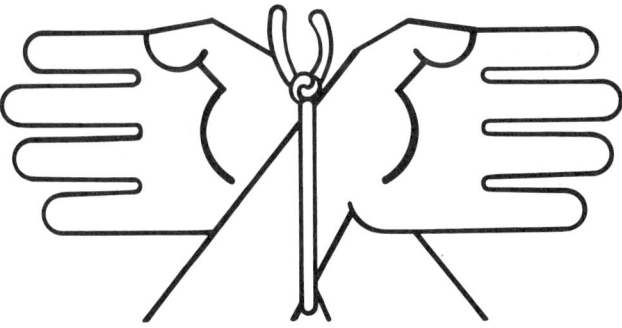

Seller beware

through the process of qualifying a buyer. You need to understand that while we will explain some important steps in how to do this, you still may not want to. In that case, it is often possible to hire a commercial lender to evaluate the loan for you. The way this is done is to complete the negotiations with your prospective buyer, then take the buyer's offer to purchase to a reputable commercial lender, such as a bank or savings and loan company. Request that the lender compile a properly documented loan package for you and collect the loan payments. This service will cost what might seem to be a considerable fee, but it is better than the alternative of not qualifying the buyer at all. Perhaps the least expensive alternative is to qualify the buyer yourself. It is not a difficult task, and we will show you how. Let's examine each of the three steps in order.

Completion of credit form

Although some buyers may not want to complete a credit form for the owner-financed property, this initial step will go a long way toward avoiding many unfortunate business deals in real estate. You can rest assured that any commercial lender would require such a form. Remember that the advantage to the buyer generally is that the property is being sold at less interest and often with a lower down payment, which will make the purchase very attractive. But the contract typically is for a relatively large sum of money and for many years. The risk is too great not to qualify the buyer. If the buyer refuses to complete the form, find another buyer. It is as simple as that.

We have included a typical buyer credit form. There are four general types of information contained in this form:

1. buyer identification
2. income
3. assets, and

4. liabilities.

Buyer identification includes the buyer's name and address, social security number, family information, occupation, and employer. The income includes salary and income from other sources. Assets include cash and securities, personal property such as automobiles, and personal home, and other real estate properties with their monthly incomes and estimated current market values. Liabilities include consumer debt, such as that for credit cards, and major indebtedness such as a home mortgage, mortgages on other real estate, and automobile loans.

The final portion of the credit form commits the buyer to truthfulness and it gives the seller permission to check with the various sources listed on the form in order to confirm the accuracy of the information provided. See the sample form below.

Name in full _____ Social Security number _____
Age __ Married __ Single __ Separated __ Number of dependents __
Home address _____ Zip code _____ Home phone _____
Employer _____ Occupation _____ How long __
Business Address _____ Business phone _____
Monthly salary _____ Commission _____
Other Income _____ From

Previous employer _____ Occupation _____ How long __

Assets
    Bank accounts: Checking _____ Balance _____
                      Savings _____ Balance _____
    Automobiles: Make _____ Model _____ Year _____ Value _____
                    Make _____ Model _____ Year _____ Value _____
    Personal home: Present Value _____
    Other real estate (1) Address _____ Monthly G.S.I. _____ Value _____
                     (2) Address _____ Monthly G.S.I. _____ Value _____
                     (3) Address _____ Monthly G.S.I. _____ Value _____
Other assets: _____

Liabilities

	Lender	Branch	Balloon payment	Monthly payment
Home	_____	_____	_____	_____
Other real property (1)	_____	_____	_____	_____
(2)	_____	_____	_____	_____
(3)	_____	_____	_____	_____

This is a true statement of my financial condition and I hereby agree to allow this application to remain in the hands of the lender whether this loan is granted or not. I give my permission for you to contact any references, employers or creditors listed above.

_____
Signature

This credit form is completed by the buyer after the offer to purchase has been made. The seller should include in the offer-to-purchase contract a provision that acceptance of the offer is contingent upon buyer qualification. Only after your investigation should you be willing to enter into a final contract.

The credit check

There are two types of credit checks. First, you should verify the information on the buyer credit form. An easy method of verifying the buyer's personal information and income is to require a copy of the previous year's federal income tax return form. It is not unusual for commercial lenders to require tax returns from the previous two years. Also, you should call the buyer's supervisor listed on the credit form, to verify current employment and salary range.

When you contact the supervisor, you must be tactful

and explain why you are calling and the nature of your relationship with his employee. You might say something like,

> Hello, Mr. _____. I am Herman Cunningham. One of your employees, Don Anderson, recently made an offer to buy a property I am selling. On his credit form he listed your company, Valley Iron Works, as his place of employment, and he said he is making approximately $35,000 in his current position. I wanted to verify this information in order to qualify him for this purchase. We were hoping to complete the sale in 10 days, and I was hoping you could verify that he is currently employed at Valley Iron Works and the income figure he gave me is correct. Is this information correct?

Be sure to ask specifically if the information is correct and to get a specific answer.

By providing the information to the supervisor yourself you have indicated to him that the buyer gave it to you and you are not simply calling to find out personal information about one of the employees of the company without the buyer's knowledge or permission. By completing the buyer credit form, the buyer is authorizing you to contact his employer and other references, so you need not be shy or hesitant to check this information. Professional lending institutions use a written request signed by the buyer himself that is forwarded on to his employer to confirm salaries. We suggest that you follow their guidelines.

You should verify the buyer's liabilities with creditors and determine both the accuracy of the amount of the liability, monthly payments, and whether or not the buyer is current on payments.

It is less important in most cases to verify the assets listed on the buyer's credit form. If the personal information, income, and liabilities information is correct, the information related to assets is likely to be correct, since it is less sensitive. It is important, however, because it offers an indication of how well the buyer manages his or her financial resources. On the other hand, if the buyer lists an income-producing asset, such as rental property, stocks, or bonds, it should be verified as part of the earlier check on income.

Suppose that the people you call for information refuse to give it to you. You still will have the personal information from the buyer's tax form. If it is important to know the current income, which may be different from last year's salary, you simply request the buyer show you a paycheck stub. If the buyer is self-employed, you still could request tax forms, which are filed quarterly with the Internal Revenue Service.

Another possibility for a credit check may be to acquire information from a local credit bureau. The laws regulating membership of these credit bureaus may make joining either impossible or unattractive because of various regulations. Before attempting to join, you will need to consult with your attorney.

If you do join, however, the credit bureau provides a good source of information about personal credit histories of persons who are likely to buy your property. These credit bureaus have cooperative working relationships with others throughout the country, so that you can acquire from your local bureau credit histories of virtually anyone in the United States.

The information you receive from your credit bureau consists primarily of bad news. Companies generally report

1. when people are seriously behind in their debts, and when
2. companies decide people simply have quit payment.

They will also report when people request credit, but with no reference to whether it actually was extended. Of course, if the credit bureau check reveals a request for credit that you see listed on the buyer's credit form, you can assume it was granted.

While the information from the credit bureau is more limited than that on the credit form, it does provide an independent source of how well the potential buyer honors financial commitments. It is not safe to use only credit bureau information, however, and you should also rely on the information provided on the buyer credit form. In fact, given a choice of the two, under current laws, an informed seller may use only a buyer credit form. On the other hand, you will want to consider the possibility of joining a credit bureau. They are relatively inexpensive to join, and the information can be valuable.

Even if you do belong to a credit bureau and the report on your potential buyer appears to be good, you must still be careful. Typically, persons selling property on contract do not belong to bureaus and would not report slow or nonpayment of loans. Think about it. The typical buyer who would default generally has a choice of which debt to forego. Which debt is likely to be defaulted on? Right, the uniform real estate contract. If you are considering selling to a buyer purchasing other properties on contract, be sure to verify the buyer's credit worthiness with these sellers.

Evaluation of information

When you evaluate the information provided in your credit check, there are two general classes of information. The first class falls under what might be termed "red flags." If you get information that falls in this category, you will want to stop any further negotiations until you are satisfied that the problem can be resolved in some way. Some of the problems simply may not be resolved. In that case, you will not want to enter into the sale. Find a new buyer.

These red flags may be listed as follows:

1. Any untrue statement on the buyer credit form.
2. Bankruptcies and lawsuits. The worst problem arises in current pending bankruptcies and lawsuits, because if the buyer loses, your property

could be entangled in a web of legal proceedings taking months, even years, to conclude. In some cases, especially bankruptcies, you could take a severe loss on the property as a result of such proceedings. Bankruptcies that already have been concluded may not be as dangerous to you directly, but they do indicate a history of poor financial management by the buyer.

3. Ratio of house payment to gross monthly income of more than 28%. If you divide the monthly house payment that the buyer has, or will have if he or she is buying a house from you, by the gross monthly income, and the ratio is greater than .28, then professional lenders conclude that it is unlikely that the buyer will be able to afford the property. The bite taken by the mortgage simply is too big to manage.

4. Ratio of total debts to gross monthly income of more than 35%. For the same reasons as for too high a mortgage payment, you will want to avoid selling your property to someone with debts greater than the 35% of his or her gross monthly income.

5. A buyer of less than the legal age in your state, generally 18, unless a qualified cosigner enters into the contract with the youth. In this case, you will want to do a credit evaluation of the cosigner as well. The danger of selling to an underage person is that the sale can be declared void, jeopardizing your interest in the sale. Various legal complications can arise, some of which could even threaten loss of the property and further collections.

6. Garnishment of wages, repossession of property, foreclosures, or deficiency judgments (court obligating the person to pay a debt). Any one of these items indicates probably irresponsibility in meeting financial obligations. Unless extremely extenuating circumstances can be substantiated,

you will want to avoid selling to a potential buyer with such a record.

Of course, you may decide to go ahead with a sale, even when one or more of the red flags is present. As long as you are satisfied that the red flag poses no real danger such a decision may be okay. It is important, however, at least to be aware of possible dangers and to address these issues before the sale, rather than to discover information at some future time that would have either prompted you not to sell or to change your negotiation strategy and contract provision.

The second type of credit information that you will want to evaluate includes a number of other considerations regarding the potential buyer's credit worthiness. These items may not set off alarms or send up red flags, such as those we discussed above. They are, however, important to your reaching a final judgment on the sale. These considerations include the following:

1. the buyer's history of late or delinquent accounts with other creditors
2. the buyer's age—generally, the older the better, except that in any case you will want the buyer to purchase credit life insurance to cover the mortgage in the event of death before fulfillment of the contract
3. martial status—generally, a married person is a better credit risk, all other things being equal
4. length of time at the buyer's present home address—normally the longer the better
5. time on the job

By examining all of these considerations, both the red-flag-type information and the additional considerations, you will develop a reasonably good profile of your potential buyer. This profile certainly can help you make a more informed decision. Also, if you have more than one offer on your property, by comparing profiles of different buyers, you can be more systematic in your analysis regarding which offer to accept.

Professionally serviced contracts

If this process of qualifying the buyer yourself sounds like more than you are willing to do, perhaps you will want to choose the option we mentioned before. Commercial lenders offer their services in such cases. Here is what you get: The lender will

1. complete a credit evaluation of the buyer
2. arrange for mortgage insurance on the buyer, protecting you if the loan is defaulted
3. collect the monthly payments for you
4. arrange for an appraisal of the property to calculate the amount of insurance and to confirm the fairness of the price of the property for the buyer.

Of course, you will have to pay for this service, but the advantages of such an arrangement may seem worth it.

The advantages to you, as the seller, are substantial. You will receive a professional credit review. You will not have to worry about the monthly collections routine many sellers are burdened with, and since the buyer is actually making payments to the financial institution, defaults on payments probably are less likely. The documentation of the loan will conform to standard legal practices in your state, thereby protecting both you and the seller. Plus, if you decide to sell the contract at some future time, the uniform documentation will make it more attractive to your potential buyers. Finally, mortgage insurance helps protect you against default.

The buyer also acquires some advantages in the arrangement. Since an appraisal is required on the property, the buyer can evaluate the fairness of its price. Also, since some sellers may conduct their business affairs in a very unprofessional manner (losing checks, requesting early payments, and the like), the buyer can be assured of dealing directly with a professional collector who will manage the financial arrangements of the loan. This can be a comfort to many buyers, who prefer the advantages of both owner financing and the professionalism of financial institutions.

In exchange for this service, you can expect to pay in the neighborhood of 2% of the total loan amount. For example, a loan of $75,000 would require approximately $1,500 for such specialized services from a commercial lender. While this may seem a large sum, many sellers prefer it when they compare lawyer fees of $100–$150 per hour to help collect defaulted loans or payments from the estates of buyers who die before a loan is paid.

We have offered a choice, either to qualify the buyer yourself or to hire a commercial lender to do it for you. As we have insisted throughout this chapter, regardless of how you choose to do it, you certainly will want to qualify any potential buyer. The risks are too great not to.

Selling the tough property

Suppose the worst. You bought a property, now want to sell it, and you have realized some severe problems that make selling it extremely difficult, if not impossible. Perhaps the problems existed when you bought the property, perhaps not. Perhaps you knew about them, but did not anticipate the devastating effect they would have upon trying to resell it. Some buyers have been in such a rush to begin a real estate investment career that their better judgment seemed to have left them when they did buy. Others, because of their inexperience, simply did not see the problems. Whatever the reason, some previous buyers are now sellers of apparently unwanted properties.

Most of these problems can be classified under five general categories:

15

1. neighborhood
2. specific location
3. exterior design
4. interior design and floorplan
5. structural damage to property

Of these five categories, by far the most important are the first two. While an ugly building, impossible floor plan, or structural damage may be very expensive to fix, they can be fixed; or at least the effects can be minimized with some careful redecorating and/or remodeling, sometimes even at relatively little expense. On the other hand, if a property is in an undesirable neighborhood or if it is located across from a drive-in movie, bordered by a 24-hour, self-service gas station on one side and a fast food restaurant on the other side, there is nothing you can do about it. Because of the extreme prob-

This little piggy went to market

lems associated with the first two categories, we will focus most of our attention in this chapter on those factors. We will address the other three more briefly.

Neighborhood/location

The point here is that you can't change the address of the property. Often, because of where a property is, you may not be able to find a ready buyer easily. Even when the property is in good repair and well decorated, you may find that few, if any, prospects will tour your property, simply because of its location. You never really get past the first telephone call with any of your prospects. This is a trap often encountered with what we earlier called handyman specials. Investors are encouraged to buy these properties so they can fix them up and sell them at a profit. A frequent problem is that the properties are generally found in undesirable neighborhoods, and, regardless of how well they are fixed up, nobody wants them.

So what do you do with a property no one seems to want because of either the neighborhood or its specific street location? Essentially you have three things to work with—condition, price, and exposure. We will assume that the condition of the property is better than any of the surrounding properties. If it isn't you will need to have some work done so that it will be. Otherwise you probably will sit on the property for a long time. With the property in good condition, you will want to price it at or below other properties on the market in the same area. You may take a loss, but the loss will be less if you do sell than if you don't. In this case, it is usually a matter of choosing the least undesirable of two bad choices. So, lower your price. If you realized at the time you bought the property that it had problems and you were able to get a really low price yourself, then you may be able to fix it up, set a low price, and still make a profit, just not as much as you think you should based upon how much you put into the property. Our best advice is to take your profit and invest in something else, if you want.

If you did not get such a good deal when you bought the property, again, take your loss and move on. The lesson you will have learned is to *buy and sell location* in the future.

Suppose the property is in good condition and your price is right. You still can't sell it if no one will look at it. This problem may be the toughest of all to solve.

One investor we know recently found a unique way of maximizing the exposure of a condominium he purchased and remodeled in a large complex. He had been able to buy four of the condominiums at very low prices, and, even though they were in one of the most undesirable locations in the city, he decided to risk the purchases anyway. His first step was to completely remodel one of the units, spending more than $5,000. The result was a high quality, fashionable, housing unit that was comparable to those in the nicer areas of the city. Next, he priced the property at more than $1,000 less than a neighboring unit in the same complex without the improvements.

The problem then was to show the condominium. His strategy was unique. He advertised in the local newspapers for a real estate agent. His advertisement read as follows:

> Wanted—Real Estate Agent. I am ready to sell my condo. I need your help. (telephone number).

When the various agents telephoned, the investor insisted they must see the property before they decided if they wanted to list it. He wound up showing the condo to four agents out of seven who called. Each commented on how unusually attractive the unit was and what a great buy it would be.

As a result of this strategy, each of the agents went back to his or her offices, telling others there what a great buy the condominium would be. After all, where else could anyone buy a luxury condominium for less than half the price. What made the property even more attractive was the fact that the investor would be improving the other three units in the same complex, probably prompting other owners to do likewise. The result would be a significantly upgraded property. The enthusiasm spread among the agents, who actively pursued the listing. When the investor did choose an agent, a representative of a large firm, 25 more agents toured the property from that firm. At that point, the unit had been exposed to four agencies in the city, all with an on-site tour of the unit, and every agent in one firm had seen the property.

All responses were highly favorable with respect to the condominium. Because of its value, even though the property had an undesirable location, as many agents were actively trying to sell that property as any other in the city at the time. It will be even easier for the investor to sell the next three condominiums. The key to this success story is exposure. Perhaps you may have to take a loss, whereas this investor made a profit. At least you will be more likely to sell with such a strategy. Of course, there are no guarantees this strategy will work every time, but it makes sense that if you have a better product for significantly less money and people know about it, you are more likely to be able to sell it than if your product is undistinguished, is overpriced, and no one either knows or cares.

Property design and condition

In this section we discuss the last three of the five general categories of tough problems to solve. If your property has a bad interior or exterior design or is in bad condition you have a choice—fix it or eat it, maybe both. Not much good will come from doing nothing at all. If you do nothing, the result likely will be that people simply will not buy it. Realistically, it is generally much wiser to repair, remodel, or cover the problem, or if not, to either sell the property at a give-away price or hold on and wait. If the problem is one of run-down condition, you probably will be able to sell the property more easily if you repair it. In fact, you likely will minimize your losses even if you have to fix relatively expensive problems, like faulty plumbing, a bad roof, or a cracked or slipping foundation.

If the problem is one of exterior design, you may want to remodel. For example, some older homes do not have driveways, carports or garages. If the potential buyers in your neighborhood turn away because of lack of these conveniences, you probably will want to install a driveway and carport or garage. Some homes in the western United States have rock gardens instead of grass lawns. Some of these rock gardens do not seem to appeal to anyone but the owners who built them. Their appearance can destroy even an otherwise attractive house. One house we know appears almost normal in most respects, except that on the four outer corners are castle turrets sticking high above the roof line. Not many people would want these turrets even if they like the rest of the house. By restructuring the roof line, the turrets could be eliminated and the little rooms at each corner could be used productively in various ways.

When do you draw the line and say you can't afford to fix a problem? This depends upon your economic circumstance and the ultimate selling price of the home. Remember that you are trying to minimize your losses. If you have to spend too much to fix a problem, you may find that it would have been cheaper to have done nothing at all. Of course, this decision is a matter of judgment. A current rule of thumb among some real estate investors we know is that if a problem costs more than about 10% of the home's value without the problem, consider it unfixable and slash prices just to get rid of the property. Surprisingly, even experienced investors make bad purchases on occasion. If you decide not to fix the problems, call your property a handyman special and emphasize how much fun it will be to fix it up.

The same rule of thumb holds for interior design problems, but there are other things you can do to minimize what otherwise might seem to be an unfixable interior design problem. Creative interior decorators can do wonders to draw attention from floorplan problems, and, in some cases, they even can convert some of these problems into unique pluses. We are reminded of a home with an almost unbearably small bedroom with a very small closet. The owner hired an artist to paint a rainbow across the wall opposite the entry. Not one person interested in the house commented on how small the room was. Everyone commented on the beautiful rainbow.

Perhaps, with the information in this chapter, you may even be lucky enough to see your property as the maturing ugly duckling becoming a beautiful swan, rather than as a real turkey. Regardless of how you see it, it should be easier to sell.

The time value of money

One of the most valuable skills you need for the real estate business is an understanding of the time value of money, especially the present-value concept. The basic idea is that time is worth money. Given a choice most people would rather receive a dollar today rather than receive it a year from now. If you receive it today you can invest it so that it can earn interest and accumulate to more than one dollar after the year has passed. That is the reason that when you borrow money you pay back more than you receive. The difference is interest, which is the cost of the time that you use the money before returning it.

Suppose, for example, that you borrow $1,000 on January 1, 1984. You promise to pay it back on December 31, 1984, plus 12% interest. At the end of the year you will pay

16

back $1,120, which represents the $1,000 you borrowed plus $120 (.12 × 1000) interest. The same principle holds when you have a series of monthly payments. Suppose you must pay back the $1,000 loan in 12 monthly payments. Assume again that the annual interest rate is 12%, which is 1% per month for each of the 12 monthly payments. Your monthly payments will be $88.85, which will total $1,066.20 ($88.85 × 12 monthly payments) for the full year. The difference between these total payments and the $1,000 borrowed represents the interest charged for lending the money. It is the amount you paid for the use of the money during the year.

But notice that even though you borrowed $1,000 in both cases, the total amount you paid back was not the same. Actually, by paying back part of the money each month, you did not use all of it all year. Consequently, you were not charged as much interest. When you borrowed $1,000 and

Scrooge's delight

paid it all back at the end of the year, you paid $120 interest ($1,120–$1,000), and when you made monthly payments, you paid $66 interest.

Perhaps you are asking yourself, "How can I calculate exactly how much the payments are supposed to be for different interest rates?" Good question. You use the following formula and interest tables (contained in the present value table at the end of the chapter, starting on page 142).

$$\frac{\text{Amount borrowed}}{\text{Interest table figure}} = \text{Amount of monthly payment}$$

Let's use our example above to calculate the monthly payment. The amount borrowed was $1,000. In the interest tables, on page 144, you will see different interest rates across the top of the page and you will see the number of periods listed down the left column of the page. In our example you were making payments for one year, therefore the number of periods is one. The yearly interest rate was established at 12%. Find the column for 12% interest across the top of the present value table, which is the 4th column, page 144. The number in the table in the 4th column at the 1st row is 11.255077. We now can calculate the monthly payment amount:

$$\frac{\$1,000}{11.255077} = \$88.85$$

Suppose you contracted to pay back the $1,000 over five years in 60 monthly payments. Since we are using the 12% interest rate, stay in the same column but you will find the number in the 5th row. The number in the table in the 12% column at the 5th row is 44.955038. Consequently, your monthly payment for the five-year pay period would be calculated as follows:

$$\frac{\$1,000}{44.955038} = \$22.24$$

The total payments in this case would be $22.24 × 60, or $1,334.40. That would be the original $1,000 loan, plus $334.40 in interest.

Let's take another example where you borrowed $125,000 at 14% interest on a 30-year note, and payments are due monthly. The number of years would be 30. The number in the table corresponding to 30 years at 14% per year would be 84.397320. The monthly payment, then, would be calculated as follows:

$$\frac{\$125,000}{84.397320} = \$1,481.09$$

The total payments would be $1,481.09 × 360, or $533,192.40.

Suppose, however, that the only information that you are given is the monthly payment and the interest rate. How can you compute how much money actually is being borrowed? A similar formula will help make this computation:

Monthly payment × Interest table figure = Amount borrowed

Assume you are buying a duplex from a seller, who has asked no money down and $1,000 per month for 20 years, or 240 months, at 12% annual interest rate. As before, there are 12 monthly payments per year. The number in the table corresponding to 12% interest for 12 years is 90.189416. The amount of the loan is calculated as follows:

90.819416 × 1,000 = $90,819.42

The amount of the loan represents the cash price of the property in this case.

Suppose now that you find a property that requires $25,000 down and $800 a month for 20 years or 240 months, at 12% interest. What is the cash price of the property?

90.819416 × 800 = $72,655.53

The cash price of the property, then, is the amount borrowed,

$72,655.53, plus the $25,000 down payment, or a total of $97,655.53.

The property has one present value at 12% interest but there are two components of the figure. First, the down payment of $25,000 and second, the stream of payments of $800 that will continue for 20 years. We must determine what is the present value of each component and then combine the two present values for a total present value. Beginning with the down payment, if it is paid today it has a present value equal to its face value of $25,000. Add to this amount the present value of $800 for 240 months at 12% interest. The table on page 144 will help us determine the present value of the payment stream. The year on the left side is 20 and the interest rate across the top of the table 12%. The table figure is 90.819416.

The present value of the payments is:

90.819416 × $800 = $72,655.53

The total price of the property is then equal to the $25,000 cash down payment and the $72,655.53, or $97,655.53.

Let's complicate the transaction slightly more. Suppose we buy a property for $100,000. The seller offers us the following terms: $25,000 as a down payment, and 12% interest on the remaining balance with payments due each month, as if the payments were to be paid over 30 years. After the end of the fifth year, however, the seller requires a balloon payment of the entire unpaid balance. What is the present cash price for the property at a 12% discount or interest rate? The total discounted cash price in this case is the sum of

1. the down payment,
2. the present cash equivalent value of the monthly payments, calculated as before, and
3. the present cash value of the balloon payment.

The first thing we need to calculate is the required monthly payment that will amortize the $75,000 loan at 12%

interest as if it were being paid over 30 years. On page 146, we find the number .01028613. It is across from row 30 and down from the 12% interest column.

.01028613 × $75,000 = $771.45

The next step is to determine what will be the unpaid balance of the loan at the end of the five years. To do this we multiply the monthly payment ($771.45) by 94.946551. This figure is from page 144. If 5 years have expired from the original 30 years then 25 more years are necessary to fully amortize the loan, but the seller asked for the balance to be paid in full at the end of the fifth year. The balloon is equal to the present value of the remaining monthly payments discounted at the contract interest rate of 12%. Find the 25 year row on the chart and the 12% column on page 144. The number is 94.946551.

The balance at the end of the fifth year is:

94.946551 × $771.45 = $73,246.52

Now we know the three elements:

1. the cash down payment of $25,000
2. $771.45 per month for 5 years
3. balloon payment of $73,246.52 in 5 years.

All we need to do is determine the present value of each and combine them to arrive at the total present value of the property using a 12% interest rate. The present value of the monthly payment stream is figured like the one in the previous example. For this solution turn to page 144 of the appendix and find the number corresponding to row 5 and the 12% interest column. The number is 44.955038. The present value of the monthly payments is figured as follows:

44.955038 × $771.45 = $34,680.56

The present value of the balloon payment is as simple

as our first example except the amount is due in 5 years instead of one year. Therefore, the value today is less than it will be in five years. Calculate its present value as before. The equation factor is found on page 142, row 5 and column 12%, .55045.

The present value of the $73,246.52 is $40,318.54.

.55045 × $73,246.52 = $40,318.54

The present value of the contract is the total of all three of the present values:

$25,000	p.v. of the down payment
$34,680.56	p.v. of the 60 monthly payments
$40,318.54	p.v. of the balloon payment in 5 years
$99,999,10	

It is not a coincidence that the present value of the three items is almost exactly equal to our beginning price of $100,000. Since the contract was written using 12% interest and we also used 12% interest in our discounting of the cash flows, the present values are essentially equal.

Suppose the same payments, but using different interest rates. For example, in 1981, it was possible to invest cash in bank notes that would earn 14% interest or more. If it were possible to achieve a 14% rate of return on a low risk investment then we would require more than that on a risky investment, perhaps 16 or 18%.

Now if we were to determine the present value of our last example using a 16% interest factor our new present value would be lower than the $100,000. Let's try it.

First, the present value of the down payment is still $25,000.

Second, the present value of the 60 payments of $771.45 is $31,723.33. Turn to page 145 and find line 5 and the 16% column. The corresponding number is 41.121706.

41.121706 × $771.45 = $31,723.33

Third, the balloon payment remains the same amount but we will use a different factor to find its present value. Multiply the $73,246.52 by .451711 which is found on page 143, line 5, column 16%.

.451711 × $73,246.52 = $33,086.25

Our total present value using 16% interest is:

$25,000.00
$31,723.33
$33,086.25
$89,809.58

This chapter has discussed the time value of money, with several illustrations. Very likely, few readers will grasp the material in this chapter on the first reading. Do not be discouraged if you need several readings of the chapter to be able to manage the calculations. The effort will be worth it. We promise.

Numerous hand-held calculators now are available that will make these computations automatically. If you find that you need to make such calculations regularly, you probably will want to invest in one of these calculators and study the owner's manual carefully.

Present value of $1

Year	9.00%	10.00%	11.00%	12.00%	13.00%
1	.914238	.905212	.896283	.887449	.878710
2	.835831	.819410	.803323	.787566	.772130
3	.764149	.741740	.720005	.698925	.678478
4	.698614	.671432	.645329	.620260	.596185
5	.638700	.607789	.578397	.550450	.523874
6	.583924	.550178	.518408	.488496	.460333
7	.533845	.498028	.464640	.433515	.404499
8	.488062	.450821	.416449	.384723	.355437
9	.446205	.408089	.373256	.341422	.312326
10	.407937	.369407	.334543	.302995	.274444
11	.372952	.334392	.299846	.268892	.241156
12	.340967	.302696	.268747	.238628	.211906
13	.311725	.274004	.240873	.211771	.186204
14	.284991	.248032	.215890	.187936	.163619
15	.260549	.224521	.193499	.166783	.143774
16	.238204	.203240	.173430	.148012	.126336
17	.217775	.183975	.155442	.131353	.111012
18	.199099	.166536	.139320	.116569	.097548
19	.182024	.150751	.124870	.103449	.085716
20	.166413	.136462	.111919	.091806	.075319
21	.152141	.123527	.100311	.081473	.066184
22	.139093	.111818	.089907	.072303	.058156
23	.127164	.101219	.080582	.064165	.051103
24	.116258	.091625	.072225	.056944	.044904
25	.106288	.082940	.064734	.050534	.039458
26	.097172	.075078	.058020	.044847	.034672
27	.088839	.067962	.052002	.039799	.030467
28	.081220	.061520	.046609	.035320	.026771
29	.074254	.055688	.041775	.031345	.023524
30	.067886	.050410	.037442	.027817	.020671

Present value of $1

Year	14.00%	15.00%	16.00%	18.00%	20.00%
1	.870063	.861509	.853045	.836387	.820081
2	.757010	.742197	.727686	.699544	.672534
3	.658646	.639409	.620749	.585090	.551532
4	.573064	.550856	.529527	.489362	.452301
5	.498601	.474568	.451711	.409296	.370924
6	.433815	.408844	.385330	.342330	.304188
7	.377446	.352223	.328704	.286321	.249459
8	.328402	.303443	.280399	.239475	.204577
9	.285730	.261419	.239193	.200294	.167769
10	.248603	.225214	.204042	.167523	.137585
11	.216301	.194024	.174057	.140114	.112831
12	.188195	.167153	.148479	.117190	.092530
13	.163742	.144004	.126659	.098016	.075882
14	.142466	.124061	.108046	.081979	.062230
15	.123954	.106879	.092168	.068567	.051033
16	.107848	.092078	.078624	.057348	.041852
17	.093834	.079326	.067069	.047965	.034322
18	.081642	.068340	.057213	.040118	.028147
19	.071034	.058875	.048806	.033554	.023082
20	.061804	.050722	.041633	.028064	.018930
21	.053773	.043697	.035515	.023472	.015524
22	.046786	.037645	.030296	.019632	.012731
23	.040707	.032432	.025844	.016420	.010440
24	.035417	.027940	.022046	.013733	.008562
25	.030815	.024071	.018806	.011486	.007021
26	.026811	.020737	.016043	.009607	.005758
27	.023328	.017865	.013685	.008035	.004722
28	.020296	.015391	.011674	.006721	.003873
29	.017659	.013260	.009958	.005621	.003176
30	.015365	.011423	.008495	.004701	.002604

Present value of $1 per period

Year	9.00%	10.00%	11.00%	12.00%	13.00%
1	11.434 913	11.374 508	11.314 565	11.255 077	11.196 042
2	21.889 146	21.670 855	21.455 619	21.243 387	21.034 112
3	31.446 805	30.991 236	30.544 874	30.107 505	29.678 917
4	40.184 782	39.428 160	38.691 421	37.973 959	37.275 190
5	48.173 374	47.065 369	45.993 034	44.955 038	43.950 107
6	55.476 849	53.978 665	52.537 346	51.150 391	49.815 421
7	61.153 965	60.236 667	58.402 903	56.648 453	54.969 328
8	68.258 439	65.901 488	63.660 103	61.527 703	59.498 115
9	73.839 382	71.029 355	68.372 042	65.857 790	63.477 604
10	78.941 693	75.671 163	72.595 275	69.700 522	66.974 419
11	83.606 420	79.872 986	76.380 487	73.110 752	70.047 103
12	87.871 092	83.676 528	79.773 109	76.137 157	72.747 100
13	91.770 018	87.119 542	82.813 859	78.822 939	75.119 613
14	95.334 564	90.236 201	85.539 231	81.206 434	77.204 363
15	98.593 409	93.057 439	87.981 937	83.321 664	79.036 253
16	101.572 769	95.611 259	90.171 293	85.198 824	80.645 952
17	104.296 613	97.923 008	92.133 576	86.864 707	82.060 410
18	106.786 856	100.015 633	93.892 337	88.343 095	83.303 307
19	109.063 531	101.099 902	95.468 685	89.655 089	84.395 453
20	111.144 954	103.624 619	96.881 539	90.819 416	85.355 132
21	113.047 870	105.176 801	98.147 856	91.852 698	86.198 412
22	114.787 589	106.581 856	99.282 835	92.769 683	86.939 409
23	116.378 106	107.853 730	100.300 098	93.583 461	87.590 531
24	117.832 218	109.005 045	101.211 853	94.305 647	88.162 677
25	119.161 622	110.047 230	102.029 044	94.946 551	88.665 428
26	120.377 014	110.990 629	102.761 478	95.515 321	89.107 200
27	121.488 172	111.844 604	103.417 947	96.020 075	89.495 389
28	122.504 035	112.617 635	104.006 328	96.468 019	89.836 495
29	123.432 776	113.317 392	104.533 685	96.865 546	90.136 227
30	124.281 866	113.950 820	105.006 346	97.218 331	90.399 605

Present value of $1 per period

Year	14.00%	15.00%	16.00%	18.00%	20.00%
1	11.137 455	11.079 312	11.021 609	10.907 505	10.795 113
2	20.827 743	20.624 235	20.423 539	20.030 405	19.647 986
3	29.258 904	28.847 267	28.443 811	27.660 684	26.908 062
4	36.594 546	35.931 481	35.285 465	34.042 554	32.861 916
5	42.977 016	42.034 592	41.121 706	39.380 269	37.744 561
6	48.530 168	48.292 474	46.100 283	43.844 283	41.748 727
7	53.361 760	51.822 185	50.347 235	47.578 633	45.032 470
8	57.565 549	55.724 570	53.970 077	50.701 675	47.725 406
9	61.223 111	59.086 509	57.060 524	53.313 749	49.933 833
10	64.405 420	61.982 847	59.696 816	55.498 454	51.744 924
11	67.174 230	64.478 068	61.945 692	57.325 714	53.230 165
12	69.583 269	66.627 722	63.864 085	58.854 011	54.448 184
13	71.679 284	68.479 668	65.500 561	60.132 260	55.447 059
14	73.502 950	70.075 134	66.896 549	61.201 371	56.266 217
15	75.089 654	71.449 643	68.087 390	62.095 562	56.937 994
16	76.470 187	72.633 794	69.103 231	62.843 452	57.488 906
17	77.671 337	73.653 950	69.969 789	63.468 978	57.940 698
18	78.716 413	74.532 823	70.709 003	63.992 160	58.311 205
19	79.625 696	75.289 980	71.339 585	64.429 743	58.615 050
20	80.416 829	75.942 278	71.877 501	64.795 732	58.864 229
21	81.105 164	76.504 237	72.336 367	65.101 841	59.068 575
22	81.704 060	76.988 370	72.727 801	65.357 866	59.236 156
23	82.225 136	77.405 455	73.061 711	65.572 002	59.373 585
24	82.678 506	77.764 777	73.346 552	65.751 103	59.486 289
25	83.072 966	78.074 336	73.589 534	65.900 901	59.578 715
26	83.416 171	78.341 024	73.796 809	66.026 190	59.654 512
27	83.714 781	78.570 778	73.973 623	66.130 980	59.716 672
28	83.974 591	78.768 713	74.124 454	66.218 625	59.767 648
29	84.200 641	78.939 236	74.253 120	66.291 930	59.809 452
30	84.397 320	79.086 142	74.362 878	66.353 242	59.843 735

Mortgage constant to amortize
(monthly payments)

Year	9.00%	10.00%	11.00%	12.00%	13.00%
1	.08745148	.08791589	.08838166	.08884879	.08931728
2	.04568474	.04614493	.04660784	.04707347	.04754182
3	.03179973	.03226719	.03273872	.03321431	.03369395
4	.02488504	.02536258	.02584552	.02633384	.02682750
5	.02075836	.02124704	.02174242	.02224445	.02275307
6	.01802554	.01852584	.01903408	.01955019	.02007411
7	.01608908	.01660118	.01712244	.01765273	.01819196
8	.01465020	.01517416	.01570843	.01625284	.01680726
9	.01354291	.01407869	.01462586	.01518423	.01575359
10	.01266758	.01321507	.01377500	.01434709	.01493107
11	.01196080	.01251988	.01309235	.01367788	.01427611
12	.01138031	.01195078	.01253555	.01313419	.01374625
13	.01089681	.01147848	.01207527	.01268666	.01331210
14	.01048938	.01108203	.01169054	.01231430	.01295264
15	.01014267	.01074605	.01136597	.01200168	.01265242
16	.00984516	.01045902	.01109000	.01173725	.01239988
17	.00958804	.01021210	.01085381	.01151216	.01218614
18	.00936445	.00999844	.01065050	.01131950	.01200433
19	.00916897	.00981259	.01047464	.01115386	.01184898
20	.00899726	.00965022	.01032188	.01101086	.01171576
21	.00884581	.00950780	.01018871	.01088700	.01160114
22	.00871174	.00938246	.01007223	.01077938	.01150226
23	.00859268	.00927182	.00997008	.01068565	.01141676
24	.00848664	.00917389	.00988027	.01060382	.01134267
25	.00839196	.00908701	.00980113	.01053224	.01127835
26	.00830723	.00900977	.00973127	.01046952	.01122244
27	.00823125	.00894098	.00966950	.01041449	.01117376
28	.00816300	.00887960	.00961480	.01036613	.01113133
29	.00810158	.00882477	.00956629	.01032359	.01109432
30	.00804623	.00877572	.00952323	.01028613	.01106200

Mortgage constant to amortize
(monthly payments)

Year	14.00%	15.00%	16.00%	18.00%	20.00%
1	.08978712	.09025831	.09073086	.09167999	.09263451
2	.04801288	.04848665	.04896311	.04992410	.05089580
3	.03417763	.03466533	.03515703	.03615240	.03716358
4	.02732648	.02783075	.02834028	.02937500	.03043036
5	.02326825	.02378993	.02431806	.02539343	.02649388
6	.02060574	.02114501	.02169184	.02280779	.02395283
7	.01874001	.01929675	.01986206	.02101784	.02220620
8	.01737150	.01794541	.01852879	.01972321	.02095320
9	.01633370	.01692434	.01752525	.01875689	.02002650
10	.01552664	.01613350	.01675131	.01801852	.01932557
11	.01488666	.01550915	.01614317	.01744418	.01878634
12	.01437127	.01500877	.01565825	.01699120	.01836609
13	.01395103	.01460287	.01526704	.01663001	.01803522
14	.01360490	.01427040	.01494845	.01633950	.01777265
15	.01331741	.01399587	.01468701	.01610421	.01756297
16	.01307699	.01376770	.01447110	.01591256	.01739466
17	.01287476	.01357700	.01429188	.01575573	.01725903
18	.01270383	.01341691	.01414247	.01562691	.01714936
19	.01255876	.01328198	.01401746	.01552078	.01706046
20	.01243521	.01316790	.01391256	.01543312	.01698825
21	.01232967	.01307117	.01382430	.01536055	.01692948
22	.01223929	.01298897	.01374990	.01530038	.01688158
23	.01216173	.01291899	.01368706	.01525041	.01684251
24	.01209504	.01285929	.01363391	.01520887	.01681060
25	.01203761	.01280831	.01358889	.01517430	.01678452
26	.01198808	.01276470	.01355072	.01514551	.01676319
27	.01194532	.01272738	.01351833	.01512151	.01674574
28	.01190836	.01269540	.01349082	.01510149	.01673146
29	.01187639	.01266797	.01346745	.01508479	.01671977
30	.01184872	.01264444	.01344757	.01507085	.01671019

Buying and selling real estate contracts

An attractive alternative to investing in property is investing in real estate contracts. The following diagram illustrates how these arrangements work:

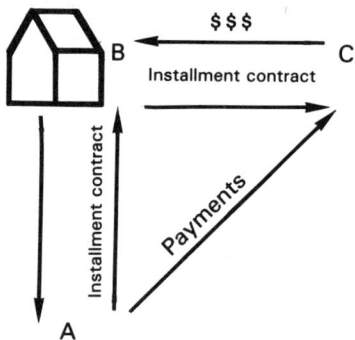

17

Party B sells a piece of property to Party A on contract. Party A keeps the property, and Party B later sells the contract to Party C. At the conclusion of the sale of the contract to Party C, Party A has the property, Party C owns the contract, and Party B is free to invest the money from the contract sale in another property. Party A then will make all future payments to Party C.

A review of the mathematics pertaining to one of these transactions will help you understand some of the advantages and disadvantages for the parties involved. If you haven't yet studied the present-value material presented in chapter 16, you should now. Your ability to understand investments in contracts depends upon a thorough understanding of discounted cash flows. Even though it may appear formidable, a concentrated effort to master that material will pay great dividends not only in these transactions, but in your real estate and other business transactions in general.

What's it worth to you?

Suppose Party B originally sells the property to A for $100,000 at 11% for 30 years. Party A paid no money down and is contracted to pay $952 a month for that period. After five years Party B sells the contract to Party C, who desires 25% return on the investment. Since the future payments to be made by Party A are fixed at $952 per month, based upon 11%, Party C will desire a discount to compensate for the difference between the 11% and the desired 25%. The discounted price for the contract with a remaining life of 25 years, is $45,617 (the present value of $952 per month for the 25 years or 300 months at 25%). The remaining principle on the contract is $97,164, however, with the difference of $51,547 being attributable to the difference in interest rates. Notice that the purchase of the contract was made for about $.47 on the $1.00.

What would prompt Party B to sell the contract at what appears to be such a tremendous loss? Basically, it boils down to the need for immediate cash. The immediate $45,617 in cash was more important than the $952 per month for the next 25 years. The immediate cash was so much more important in fact, that Party B was willing to forfeit a substantial amount of interest to get it.

We have been conservative in this example of 25% discount rate. Although discount rates may go as low as 18% in today's market, rates of 40%–50% are sometimes given, and, in extreme cases, a few contracts are sold at prices yielding to the purchaser as much as 70% interest. If we use a 70% discount rate, the purchase price of the contract for our above example would be only $16,319.

The discount rate depends upon various factors, including the age of the contract, the original sale price of the property, the down payment that was made originally, the current value of the property (both land and building), payment history by the buyer, and position of the contract (first, second, third position, and so forth, as we discussed earlier.)

An important factor affecting the amount of profits available from buying contracts is the tax effect. The profit from contracts is totally interest income, which typically is taxed at a higher rate than the capital gains income from real estate property. This difference in tax effect must also be considered when calculating a discount rate.

Even with such large discounts, many successful investors are able to find people willing to sell their contracts. These investors can make large fortunes. Why then do not all investors forget property investments and simply buy contracts? The basic reason is that it is much easier to buy real estate with little investment capital. Often no down payment is required and monthly payments may be made with rental proceeds from the purchased property. On the other hand, the purchase of a contract requires a large amount of cash, because the total price must be paid at the time of purchase. Not many people have the required cash. As profits are made on other properties, however, clever investors will be able to reinvest them in contracts, earning the higher rates of return. Remember, however, that fewer contracts than properties are available for sale. Investments in contracts require patience as well as money.

The most common method of finding contracts for sale is simply to advertise in the classified ads in the newspaper. A typical ad may be worded as follows:

> Immediate cash for real estate contracts. Call (telephone number).

Suppose you are in a position to buy a contract. What are the characteristics you look for when deciding to buy one? Our preferences, as usual, are more conservative than some investors. The following list will offer you some guidelines from this conservative point of view.

1. When the property was sold on contract, the sales price was at least equal to its estimated fair market value.
2. The buyer made a cash down payment of at least 5% of the sales price.

3. The estimated current value of the property exceeds the outstanding balance of the contract.
4. The current condition of the property is such that the estimated life of the building is greater than the remaining life of the contract. An exception may be made when the value of the land is exceptionally high in comparison with any building on the land.
5. A contract in the first position (that is, the first lien) is much to be preferred over second or third liens.
6. The sale was made at least three years before, so that the buyer can have confirmed a sound payment history.
7. The property is not decreasing in value.
8. A title search on the property shows good title and up-to-date property-tax payments.

Contracts meeting all of these requirements will sell with lower discounted interest rates, because they represent lower risk to the investor. As you relax these requirements, you will find that you can purchase contracts at substantially higher interest rates, which means much lower prices. Of course, you need to realize that by relaxing the requirements, you are increasing your risk of possible losses.

Another distinct advantage of investing in contracts is the average length of time they are held before the property is either sold or refinanced, in which case the contract normally is paid off. The national average for the length of time contracts are outstanding is much less than the original length of loan agreements, even though they are written for up to 30 years. Notice what this means for the person purchasing a five-year-old contract: The amount that the property buyer must pay is based upon the original interest rate. In our example, assume the buyer pays off the loan at the end of eight years. The balance due is $94,549. Party C, who purchased the contract, would have invested $45,617, collected $952 per month for three years, and then collected

$94,549 when Party A paid off the mortgage contract. This money is available for reinvestment by Party C.

For those persons with adequate cash, contracts offer a way to buy high-yielding real estate investments without having to actually manage properties. Certainly for many, these investments are even more attractive than more traditional alternatives in land and buildings.

Taxes

We cannot pretend to tell you in this short chapter all that you need to know about taxes affecting real estate transactions. Our best advice is to hire a good tax accountant or attorney. On the other hand, it wouldn't be fair to totally ignore taxes either. Consequently, we shall focus this discussion upon some very general principles and then upon a single, simple example involving the sale of an investment property on an installment contract.

Kinds of taxes

Basically, taxes may be categorized

1. by the taxing authority levying the tax
2. by the nature of the tax itself.

18

There are four primary taxing authorities:

- local (municipal, township, or community) governments
- county or parrish governments
- state governments
- the federal government

The different kinds of taxes include property, school, sales, and income taxes.

Local and county (parrish) governments acquire most of their revenues from property taxes. These are taxes assessed to property owners located within the boundaries of

Render unto Caesar

the government units. The taxes are fixed according to property values and are not subject to the control of the individual owner. They remain a fact of life for holders of real estate.

State governments utilize sales and income taxes. While provisions differ from state to state, sales taxes do affect rental income in some states. These taxes are computed as a specific percentage of gross rental income. Again, they are not subject to the taxpayer's control. Income taxes, however, are a different matter. State income taxes generally are based upon the amount of federal income taxes, which do provide some degree of control through tax planning.

The federal income tax related to real estate includes two types of taxes—ordinary income tax and the capital gains taxes. Very briefly, ordinary income taxes are based upon income that is generated from the operation of the property and from interest earned from the sale of a property involving installment payments over time. Capital gains taxes are charged on the property at the time of its sale and are based upon the difference between its sales price and the original purchase price, which may be adjusted for depreciation if it is an investment property.

The distinction between ordinary income and capital gains is important because capital gains can lead to lower taxes than ordinary income can. Consequently, professional investors carefully study the tax implications of their investments. This means tax planning with a knowledgeable tax accountant or attorney.

A simple example

This book is about creative financing, or owner financing, utilizing real estate contracts. The following example illustrates the tax effect on a sale of a property providing both ordinary income (through the collection of interest) and capital gains. This is the most common type of owner-financing arrangement, in which monthly payments are made for the life of the contract.

Suppose you bought a property two years ago for $100,000 and now you are selling it for $120,000. Over the two years, you took $5,000 in depreciation on the property. Therefore, the capital gain on the property is $25,000 (that is, $120,000 minus the adjusted original price of $95,000). You will pay the capital gains tax on this amount.

Suppose further that you are charging 12% interest on the contract, which will be paid over a 30-year period. The monthly payments will be $1,234.33, or $14,812.08 for the year. Of this total for the first year, only $435.51 will apply to the reduction of the principal amount of $120,000. The rest, or $14,376.57, will be interest, which is taxed at your ordinary income tax rates.

You will be expected to pay the taxes on the interest income in the year in which you collect it. Since you will not be collecting all $120,000 at once, of course, you will not be required to pay all of the capital gains tax in the year of sales. Rather, you will pay a percentage of the tax in the years you collect payment for the property. That calculation is based upon the proportion of the reduction of the principal amount of the note which can be attributed to the gain. In our example, the gain is $25,000, which is 20.8% (that is, $25,000/$120,000) of the total price. The principal reduction for the first year's payments we stated was $435.51. Of that amount, 20.8%, or $90.59, represents the capital gain accounted for in the first year and to which the capital gains tax will be applied. Of course, over the life of the contract the total $25,000 capital gain will be taxed, but it will be spread over the 30 years.

The table on the following page outlines the total annual payments for the property, the amount of the payments applied to the principal each year, the amount of this reduction in principal that is considered capital gain, the amount of interest each year, and the balance remaining at the end of each year on the $120,000 loan. Remember that the interest each year is taxed at ordinary rates, and the capital gain is taxed at different rates.

Another matter of importance to homeowners over the age of 55 is a lifetime exclusion of $125,000 gain on a family

Year	Unpaid balance	Total payment received	Interest portion	Principal portion	×	Ratio of capital gains/principal	=	Capital gains
1	119,564.49	14,812.08	14,376.57	435.51		.208		90.57
2	119,073.73	14,812.08	14,321.32	490.76		.208		102.08
3	118,520.73	14,812.08	14,259.08	553.00		.208		115.02
4	117,897.60	14,812.08	14,188.95	623.13		.208		129.61
5	117,195.44	14,812.08	14,109.92	702.16		.208		146.05
6	116,404.23	14,812.08	14,020.87	791.21		.208		164.57
7	115,512.69	14,812.08	13,920.54	891.54		.208		185.44
8	114,508.06	14,812.08	13,807.45	1,004.63		.208		208.96
9	113,376.05	14,812.08	13,680.07	1,132.01		.208		235.48
10	112,100.46	14,812.08	13,536.49	1,275.59		.208		265.32
11	110,663.08	14,812.08	13,374.70	1,437.38		.208		298.96
12	109,043.41	14,812.08	13,192.41	1,619.67		.208		336.89
13	107,218.31	14,812.08	12,986.98	1,825.10		.208		379.62
14	105,161.76	14,812.08	12,755.53	2,056.55		.208		427.76
15	102,844.39	14,812.08	12,494.71	2,317.37		.208		482.01

Year	Unpaid balance	Total payment received	Interest portion	Principal portion	×	Ratio of capital gains/ principal	=	Capital gains
16	100,233.10	14,812.08	12,200.79	2,611.29		.208		543.15
17	97,290.67	14,812.08	11,869.65	2,942.43		.208		612.03
18	93,975.05	14,812.08	11,496.46	3,315.62		.208		689.65
19	90,238.91	14,812.08	11,075.94	3,736.14		.208		777.12
20	86,028.94	14,812.08	10,602.11	4,209.97		.208		875.67
21	81,285.06	14,812.08	10,068.20	4,743.88		.208		986.73
22	75,939.53	14,812.08	9,466.55	5,345.53		.208		1,111.87
23	69,916.06	14,812.08	8,788.61	6,023.47		.208		1,252.88
24	63,128.65	14,812.08	8,024.67	6,787.41		.208		1,411.78
25	55,480.43	14,812.08	7,163.86	7,648.22		.208		1,590.83
26	46,862.21	14,812.08	6,193.86	8,618.22		.208		1,792.59
27	37,150.98	14,812.08	5,100.85	9,711.23		.208		2,019.94
28	26,208.16	14,812.08	3,869.26	10,942.82		.208		2,276.11
29	13,877.49	14,812.08	2,481.41	12,330.67		.208		2,564.78

residence from any tax whatsoever. This means that you can buy a house for $60,000, keep it for 15 years and sell it for $150,000, for a $90,000 gain. You need not report the $90,000 gain at all for income tax purposes, either as ordinary income or capital gain. The $125,000 is a once in a life time exclusion for those over 55 years of age. If the full exclusion of $125,000 is not used at the time of sale, the balance of the exclusion cannot be carried forward to apply to another sale. In this case, $35,000 of possible tax benefits will be lost. Any future gains on other family residences must be subject to capital gains tax, unless those gains are reinvested in another residence with 24 months after sale. These rules become a little tricky, so as we said, you are better off if you consult with a good tax accountant or attorney when you enter any real estate transaction. You probably will be able to sleep a little easier knowing the government is not likely to sneak up on your blind side.

As we said, this chapter is not designed to answer all of your questions about taxes, but rather, hopefully, it gave you a very brief introduction so that when you hire a tax expert you will have at least a notion of what he or she is talking about.

Other important stuff

This chapter discusses several factors that are important to buyers and sellers. While they may appear to be of less consequence than some of the previously discussed problems, they nonetheless should be carefully considered and resolved before consummation of any contractual agreements. Attention to these details is necessary for a complete and proper meeting of the minds between the buyer and the seller. So, we discuss taxes, insurances, inspections, payment structures, penalties and defaults, and title insurance.

Property Taxes

A typical earnest money contract provides that taxes be prorated for the year so that the seller assumes liability for taxes

19

up to the date of the sale and the buyer assumes liability for taxes after that date. A problem occurs because the contract does not specify the timing of the payment of the taxes, which could significantly influence the cash flows associated with the sale. Unless the timing of these payments has been resolved at the closing, the resolution may not come until months later.

For example, a buyer and seller recently agreed on a sale of a small apartment building. The taxes were estimated to be $2,800 for the year. The buyer assumed that he would pay his portion of the taxes at the end of the year and at the end of each subsequent year when the tax notice actually was issued. The seller assumed the buyer would include one-twelfth ($236) of the total estimated taxes with each monthly payment. The seller had an underlying conventional mortgage that included payment of the taxes monthly (one-

Smorgasbord

twelfth). If the tax question had not been resolved and the buyer had succeeded in delaying the tax payment, the seller would have had to pay the $236 out of his own pocket for each month from other income sources for the remainder of the year. That amount could have made the difference between the seller being able to continue making his obligation to the lending institution and to continue avoiding possible negative cash flow and possible foreclosure on the property.

Another problem arises in some states because prorations are based upon the previous year's taxes. The current year's taxes are not known until shortly before they come due. If there is a significant difference between taxes for the previous year and those for the current year, then the prorated amounts negotiated at the time of sale may not be equitable. In most states, in most years, property taxes generally increase. Informed investors consistently can provide in their contracts for an adjustment of the tax liabilities when there is a difference between the estimates and the actual taxes due. These differences can amount to sizable sums, especially when a buyer purchases several pieces of property in the same year. Remember, too, that the closer to the end of the tax year a property is purchased, the more difference it can make in the amount of adjustment. While the adjustment is included as a provision of the contract, the actual adjustment of the taxes may not be done for several months, long after the sale is completed.

Insurance

Insurance, like taxes, is prorated between the buyer and the seller according to the percentage of the year that each owns the property. Again, like taxes, a problem can arise if no provision is made in the earnest-money agreement as to how the insurance will be paid. Either the seller continues to be liable for monthly insurance payments or the buyer can secure his own insurance on the property. In the latter case the buyer does not pay the seller a proration of the insurance premium. When the buyer does pay the seller for insurance coverage, it can be paid either monthly or annually. If there is a conflict between the buyer and the seller about how the insurance will be paid, then the sale of the property may be hindered at the closing date. The remedy is simply to specify in the earnest money agreement how the insurance will be paid. This simple attention to detail helps avoid misunderstandings when the transaction is closed. The proration of taxes and insurance is added to every agreement, but what is not dealt with is how they are to be paid. You will most likely have to do that yourself.

Inspections

Many sellers do not want prospective buyers to inspect the interior of a property until a firm offer to purchase has been made. On the other hand, an inspection by the buyer will help him arrive at a more fair price.

Also, suppose the property has some serious hidden damage which would significantly change the value of the property. In this case, who is to pay for the repairs if such liability is not negotiated? An investor recently offered to purchase a property and included an inspection provision in the earnest-money agreement. The inspection revealed several thousand dollars in structural damages to the property. While the earnest money agreement provided for an inspection, it did not provide an agreement as to who would be responsible for making any needed structural repairs discovered during the inspection. As a result, disagreement between the buyer and the seller ended without consummating the purchase and sale of the property. Had the problem been addressed and resolved before the offer-to-purchase contract had been signed, the sale probably could have been completed satisfactorily for both the buyer and the seller. The problem in this case was not so much the amount of the damage, but rather the surprise it caused after negotiations had been finalized. A price had been established, both the buyer and the seller had settled the transaction in their minds, and the unexpected damage simply was more than the buyer was willing to bear.

Payment structures

Any form of payment structure other than normal down payment with a long-term amortization of equal monthly payments needs to be carefully outlined in the offer to purchase. Such provisions as balloon payments, delayed monthly payments, staggered down payments, variable interest rates, and so forth, all must be specifically detailed in the preliminary contract. Otherwise, either they must be negotiated at the closing date, or, if ignored even then, they must be resolved after the property has been sold. The longer the wait, the more expensive the problem can become.

For example, an investor wrote an earnest-money contract calling for a $28,000 down payment on a duplex of which an initial $20,000 was to be paid in October and an additional $8,000 was to be paid several months later. The contract specified only that the buyer would pay interest on the unpaid balance after subtraction of the down payment. The seller interpreted this provision to mean that interest would be paid on the loan balance including the $8,000 left on the down payment. The buyer intended to pay interest only on the balance after subtracting the total $28,000 at the October sale date. The difference in interpretation did not come to light until after the property was already sold, and the seller wound up losing the interest on the $8,000 between the payment date of $20,000 and the remaining $8,000.

Since the offer-to-purchase agreement does not specifically outline the different variations of payment structures, these provisions need to be written in careful detail to avoid misunderstandings, unexpected losses, and possible litigation.

Penalties and defaults

Provisions for penalties on late payments and foreclosure for nonpayment are not included in many standard offer-to-purchase agreements. Since the buyer and the seller have conflicting interests in these provisions, they should be resolved in the offer to purchase to avoid the inconvenience and possible disruption of the sale if left unresolved until the closing date. The buyer, of course, would prefer no penalty for late payments whatsoever; and the longer the grace period before foreclosure, the better for the buyer. Just the opposite is true for the seller, who prefers strong encouragement for prompt payments.

Even when these issues are resolved, they can pose a problem if the investor is not careful. One of the authors once bought a property and signed a contract providing a 15-day default period. He sold the building on contract providing a 30-day grace period, which ended two weeks after the 15-day period he received on the property from the previous owner. As it turned out, the buyer to whom he had sold the building consistently waited until the 30-day deadline before paying, even though a late penalty was attached. This sequence of events meant that there was a two-week delay in the cash flow. This money had been planned for use as the author's payment which was due to the previous seller on the same day as the new buyer's payment. But the fifteen additional days that the author gave the new buyer in grace period made it impossible to use the income from the property to make the required payments to the previous owner. These payments had to come from other sources, because of the timing differences in the two contracts. Although it was not a major problem, it was an unnecessary inconvenience that could have been avoided with more careful attention to the default period.

Also, although a late fee generally motivates buyers to pay on time, it may have little effect if it is not large enough to be of consequence to the buyer. Many investors have a rule of thumb of about 5% of the monthly payment as a late fee. However you make this decision, the amount should be significant enough to encourage prompt payment. The least the authors ever accept is $50 regardless of the monthly payments. The larger the payments, of course, the more the late fee should be.

Title insurance

Every real estate sale should include an abstract of title, a title report, and title insurance. The abstract of title merely represents a historical summary of everything affecting the title to the property. A title report is taken from the abstract and outlines the current condition of the title. Title insurance guarantees the findings in the abstract and report to the buyer, and it compensates the buyer for errors in the abstract that will cause future damages. Errors are not uncommon in abstracts and title reports and in their interpretations. Title insurance can protect a buyer from many of these errors, some of which even can cause the buyer to lose the property.

The provisions in many standardized owner-financing sales contracts give the seller an option to provide *either* an abstract of title *or* title insurance. Under no condition should you, as a buyer, purchase any property without title insurance. The risks are too great. When you purchase a property, you should require title insurance, not merely an abstract of title or title report.

Sometimes a buyer might want to forego title insurance, because the seller is likely to increase the price of the property and the down payment by the amount of the cost. By foregoing title insurance, the buyer might appear to be saving on both the total price and the initial cash outlay for the down payment.

One homeowner in North Carolina bought a property with what appeared to be a clean abstract of title. The abstract was prepared by a highly respected attorney in the community who had lived there for many years and was familiar with the real estate in the area. When the homeowner tried to sell the property, however, the same attorney did a new abstract and found a cloud on the title, one which involved several members of one family disputing the property's former ownership. The current homeowner had no title insurance and was forced to pay substantial legal fees far in excess of insurance in order to protect himself.

The standard owner's coverage policy normally insures against the following:

1. most matters disclosed in public records
2. parties who lack the legal qualification to sell property, such as minors, incompetents, dead persons, and forgers
3. parties who lack legal authority to sell the property, such as agents, fiduciaries, or corporations
4. lack of delivery of instruments of title to previous owners

The standard owner's coverage policy normally does not insure against:

1. problems not disclosed in public record
2. zoning, or
3. water and mineral rights

The American Land Title Association (ALTA) provides an extended coverage policy that insures all of the above, plus unrecorded mechanic's liens, unrecorded physical easements, survey information, water and mineral rights, and the rights of persons currently in physical possession of the property. This additional coverage essentially doubles the cost of the title insurance.

One investor bought a property with the standard owner's coverage policy, and later discovered that the building on the property was partially located on the lot adjacent to the one he had bought. His appeal for compensation from his title insurance failed because the standard policy does not cover that problem. The ALTA extended policy would have. On the other hand, a survey, costing much less than the extended coverage policy, would have revealed the same information. As a buyer, you must decide what coverage best suits your needs and circumstances, but you should always have title insurance. Unfortunately, many buyers and sellers are unaware of the significant problems that can arise strictly from the earnest-money agreement and the final contract.

While our survey may not be exhaustive, you should leave this chapter with the clear understanding that

1. you must pay careful attention to the details of any contracts you sign in a purchase or sale of property.
2. competent legal counsel can save you a bundle in the final analysis.

You should also understand that if you neglect the contract problems, we outline here, and others that might come to light in your own experience, the costs can wreak financial havoc with your investment.

The consummate real estate investor

The previous chapters have illustrated a basic economic principle—"There is no such thing as a free lunch." Creative financing techniques have been a great help to buyers and sellers in tough real estate markets. Sellers want to sell and conventional financing is very restrictive; so owner financing methods have filled a need in facilitating satisfactory arrangements for both buyers and sellers. What has happened, however, is that many investors have figured out ways to take advantage of a rising real estate market using numerous variations of the basic owner-financing contract. In too many cases some of these investors either have taken unfair advantage of uninformed or unsuspecting sellers or have been indirectly hurt because of inadequate study and analysis of the investment. You should have learned several general principles in this book.

20

1. An owner financed property creates a long-term business relationship between a buyer and seller. If the benefits of the arrangement appear too lopsided in favor of one of the parties, the other's financial risk may jeopardize both parties. The primary goal of both buyer and seller should be an exchange that is fair to both. Of course, you must protect your own interest, but as we have illustrated in several cases, there is good business sense in arranging the transaction so that, if you are the seller, the buyer can afford the property, and if you are the buyer, that the seller will be fairly and adequately compensated. To the extent that either party is treated unfairly in the exchange, both may be damaged.
2. Real estate can be an excellent investment, but success requires patience. If you are in too big a hurry,

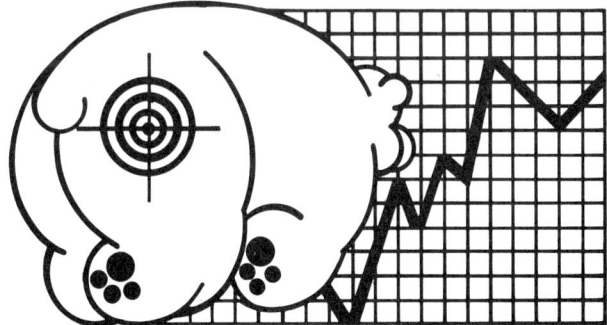

Loaded for bear

you are too likely to make some serious and costly errors. Patience can provide the seller the time and care not only to find an honest, willing buyer who can afford the property being offered, but also to make appropriate financial arrangements.

3. Patience implies that the buyer or seller has a somewhat detached and objective attitude. If he or she is too emotionally involved with the property, this emotional attachment can interfere with good judgment. An objective attitude makes a realistic analysis much easier.

4. Finally, it is difficult to successfully achieve the above three characteristics unless you are well prepared. Study and preparation are the key ingredients to successful buying and selling in real estate. We have seen investors hurt because they went to a single real estate seminar that told them to go and buy properties using very risky financial techniques. You need to understand that real estate is like other businesses. You have to study and prepare yourself if you are going to get involved. You can bet those who have their fortunes at stake prepare themselves not only in a general sense, but they also analyze each transaction carefully in order to understand every aspect of the exchange. Too much is at stake for anything less. Even if you are not an investor, perhaps your largest investment is in a home. It is a shame to see homeowners hurt because they were either uninformed or ill-informed. Careful study, with good legal counsel, can help avoid many problems costing many thousands of dollars.

Assume now that you have learned these four general principles and you are ready to either buy or sell a property. Four additional guidelines can help evaluate each proposal on the property:

1. *Shop properties*—regardless of whether you are a buyer or a seller, it pays to familiarize yourself with the market that you are entering. Buyers commonly inspect properties and compare prices, terms, location, and so forth. They get a good feel for what is available in the market. Less commonly do sellers shop the market. Such preparation can strengthen a seller's negotiating position with a buyer and increase the likelihood that a fair exchange can be arranged more quickly. This information is valuable for the seller as well as the buyer. By "shopping" properties we mean studying both properties currently on the market and those that recently have been sold. Sometimes the asking price of those on the market is significantly different from the selling price of comparable properties that actually sold.

2. *Compute and compare the numbers*—Computations help indicate the true value of the property, its associated cash flows, and future worth. While these figures may not be foolproof, they almost always offer clearer guidance than mere hunches. Also, it is a good idea to have specific criteria that properties must meet before making any commitments. These criteria help the buyer avoid being too easily persuaded by rationalizations.

3. *Structure the deal correctly*—Abide by the principles contained in this book and get competent legal counsel in order to structure the exchange to protect your interest and rights and to be sure that the contracts reflect the transaction accurately. As we have shown earlier, this critical step helps assure a more secure financial future than if you neglect it.

4. *Screen the people*—Remember that when you use owner financing you are contracting a long-term business relationship that may last as long as 30 years. In many cases it may be more important to be sure you are dealing with the right kind of

people than any other consideration. For example, we heard one investor recently say he would simply walk away from an unprofitable investment and let the seller reclaim the property and try to sue for damages. The authors would avoid any business relationship with that individual. Also, if you are buying into a contract chain, you assume a business relationship not only with the seller, but also with the other members of the chain, any one of which could create enormous legal complications for the entire chain. The point is to screen the people carefully. Even when you do screen the people with whom you do business, it is impossible to be right in your evaluations every time. Again, it is wise to employ good legal counsel in any real estate transaction to protect yourself in case of a bad judgment.

In this book we have discussed numerous specific problems relating to creative financing that you need to understand. Some of these problems have to do with your strategy of buying and selling and some of them apply directly to the contracts you will use in owner financing. The following table offers a brief outline of the problems we have discussed, along with some of the major potential dangers and our suggested remedies.

Major problems in creative financing—general guidelines

Problems	Dangers	Remedies
Negative cash flows	The property feeds off of the buyer's other income or wealth. This could cause default and loss of the property.	Structure the purchase so that there is not a negative cash flow; or be sure you can afford the negative cash flow; or do not buy the property.
Balloon payments	The buyer may be unable to meet the balloon payment when it comes due, and thus faces default.	The safest remedy is not to offer or accept a contract including a large balloon payment, unless precautions can be taken at the time of sale to assure the payment.
Contract chains	You risk losing your interest in a property because of the lack of performance by others in the chain over whom you have little or no control.	The safest remedy is not to buy or sell into a contract chain. If you do, however, follow the advice in chapter 4 on how to avoid the problems that occur.
No down payment	The buyer has no equity in the property, which substantially increases the risk of default. Also, a high probability of negative cash flows compounds the risk.	Avoid purchases and sales for no money down except in rare circumstances.
Borrowing for down payment	The same as for no down payment, except that the probability of negative cash flows increases greatly.	Avoid it either as a seller or as a buyer, except in extremely rare circumstances.

Problems	Dangers	Remedies
Inadequate earnest money	If the amount of earnest money is too little, the seller may not be adequately compensated for damages should the buyer back out.	As a seller, require enough earnest money to attract only serious buyers.
Handyman specials	It is difficult to make a profit for the novice handyman with too little money.	Leave these only to experienced persons who specialize in these kinds of properties. On the other hand, if you are capable and have enough money, have at it.
"Due on sale" clauses	Possible foreclosure because the sale of a property may not yield enough cash to pay a previous note.	Do not buy or sell a property with a "due on sale" clause in the underlying mortgage on contract unless (1) the down payment covers the liability or (2) you can get a waiver from the previous lender. In some states the law protects buyers and sellers against the "due on sale."
Double closing	High risk or theft by the buyer, and, even if not, there is a high probability of large negative cash flows created by liens in excess of the property value.	Avoid it like the plague.

Problems	Dangers	Remedies
Method of paying taxes and insurance not defined	Loss of sale or purchase due to renegotiations after an initial agreement; and possible negative cash flows.	Outline detailed provisions in the earnest money contract or in the offer to purchase and the final contract.
Payment structure undefined	Unexpected losses and possible litigation.	Outline detailed provisions in the earnest money contract and the final contract.
Penalties and defaults undefined	To the seller, the danger is possible non-payment or slow payment by the buyer.	Outline detailed provisions in the offer to purchase and final contract using shorter rather than longer periods.
Forfeiture	Possible unenforceable contract.	Use either trust deeds or at least contracts with quitclaim deeds.
Foreclosure	To the seller there might be very large financial losses, litigation, and unnecessary complications due to redemptions.	Use trust deeds as a final contract.
Title insurance	Financial losses due to unexpected title defects.	Secure adequate title insurance at the time of purchase.

Glossary

Absentee owner A person who owns property, but does not reside upon it. One who is continually away from his property and leaves its management in the care of others.

Abstract; Abstract of title A summarized, chronological complication of all the recorded instruments, and a history of ownership that has affected the title to a specific piece of land. A synopsis of its recorded documents.

Acceleration clause A clause generally found in a mortgage or installment contract stipulating that the payment of the indebtedness must be made in full in the event

---

From the *Illustrated Encyclopedic Dictionary of Real Estate*, second edition, by Jerome S. Gross (Prentice-Hall, 1978).

of a default of any of its covenants. Certain other instruments, such as bonds, leases, and notes, may also contain acceleration clauses.

Acceptance 1. Agreeing to the terms and conditions of an offer making it a binding contract. 2. The receipt of a deed constitutes automatic acceptance of title to property.

Amenities The pleasure and satisfaction gained from one's surroundings. Features, both hidden and visible, that enhance and add to the desirability of real estate. Frequently used when referring to residential properties, the word embraces the personal, human aspect of livability and pride of ownership, rather than monetary considerations.

Amortize To pay a debt in periodic amounts until the total amount, along with the interest, if any, is paid.

Appraisal Valuation. An expert opinion of the value of the property by one qualified to make such an opinion. Setting a value on an asset.

Appreciation Raising of value; increasing in worth; enhance. The opposite of *depreciation*.

As is When these words are inserted in a contract they mean that no guarantees whatsoever are given regarding the subject property. It is being purchased in exactly the condition in which it is found.

Asking price The listed price of real estate; the price at which it is formally offered in a sale. Unlike a *firm price*, the term sometimes denotes a flexible selling price; one from which negotiations can begin.

Assignee A person to whom an assignment is made or to whom a property, right, or interest is transferred.

Assignment The transfer of title or interest, in writing, from one person or group of people to another.

Assumption of mortgage Taking title to property that has an existing mortgage and being personally liable for its payments.

Balloon mortgage A mortgage that provides for periodic payments that do not completely amortize the loan at the time of its termination. As a consequence, a larger final payment becomes due.

Beneficiary A party designated in a will, trust, insurance policy, etc. to receive certain proceeds or benefits. One for whom a trust is created.

Bill of sale An instrument used in a real estate transaction when items other than real property are included in a sale. Furniture, fixtures, appliances, merchandise, motor vehicles, and similar items of personalty are found in a bill of sale.

Binder 1. A preliminary agreement in writing, with a valuable consideration given, as evidence of good faith by the offerer. It is an offer to purchase; a unilateral contract. Upon acceptance, it becomes a bilateral contract. Though it contains all the elements of a valid contract, in some areas it is considered to be temporary in nature until a more formal contract can be drawn. 2. A written instrument giving immediate insurance coverage until a regular policy can be issued.

Blanket mortgage A mortgage covering two or more pieces of property.

Book value The amount of an asset as carried on the records of a company, and not necessarily what it could bring in the open market. Book value is computed by the cost of the asset plus additions and improvements, minus accrued depreciation.

Breach of contract Not living up to the terms and conditions of a contract, refusal to carry out the provisions therein. Failure to perform without legal justification.

Broker A licensed person who, for compensation, acts as an intermediary in real estate transactions. An agent.

Buyers' market A business condition in which the type of property for sale is plentiful. Consequently, sellers are forced to lower their prices and make concessions in their terms in order to make a sale.

Capital gain Profit gained from the sale of a capital asset in excess of its appraised value.

Capitalization rate The rate of return, expressed in a percentage, that is considered a reasonable profit one should expect for his investment.

Cash flow The net income. The usable cash after all expenses are paid.

Cash value The actual money that an asset will bring on the open market without a lengthy delay. The preferred term is *market value*.

Chain of title The history of ownership, conveyances and encumbrances, both recorded and unrecorded, that have affected the title of a specific parcel of land.

Chattel Personal property.

Chattel mortgage A mortgage encumbering personal property.

Clear title Good title. Marketable title.

Close To complete a transaction; when real estate formally changes ownership. A settlement.

Closing costs The numerous expenses buyers and sellers normally incur in the transfer of ownership of real estate.

Closing statement A detailed financial account of all the credits and debits that the buyer and seller receive when completing a real estate transaction.

Cloud on title A claim, encumbrance, or apparent defect that impairs the title to real property. Any evidence appearing in the abstract which could place in dispute the *fee simple* title to the property.

Commission The fee paid a broker for his services in transaction real estate business.

Compound interest Interest computed on both the principal amount and the accruing interest as the debt matures.

Conditional sales contract A contract whereby possession is given the buyer, but title remains with the seller until certain specific conditions of the contract have been fulfilled, such as full payment of the consideration. A conditional sales contract is used primarily in an installment sales transaction, and it is variously referred to as an *installment contract, agreement for deed, contract for deed,* or a *land contract.*

Consideration Something of value given to influence a person to enter into a contract.

Contingent Dependent or conditioned upon a future event with no certainty that it will occur. It is liable to happen, but not known for sure.

Conversion The act of changing a property from one use to another, as, for example, when a residence is renovated and partitioned into offices.

Conveyance An instrument, in writing, used to transfer title to property from one to another.

Covenant An agreement between parties, written into legal instruments, in which the parties promise to do or refrain from doing certain acts.

Creditor The one to whom a debt is owed. A person who gives credit.

Credit report A report covering the credit history of a person or business.

Damages 1. Loss sustained or harm done to a person or property. 2. Loss in value to the remaining property when, under the theory of eminent domain, a portion of one's property is expropriated.

Deed An instrument under seal, signed by the grantor, transferring title to another. To be valid a deed must a) be made between competent parties, b) have a legally sound subject matter, c) contain a good and valuable consideration, d) correctly state what is being conveyed, e) be properly executed, and f) be delivered.

Default The breech of an obligation. Failure to perform the covenants of a contract.

Defective title A flaw in the title.

Deficiency judgment A judgment issued when the security for a loan is insufficient to satisfy the debt upon the loan's going into default. It is the awarding of the amount still due on a foreclosed mortgage, after applying the sum received for the sale of the property.

Depreciation 1. A lowering of value. A reduction; lessening. The decline in value of property. Loss in market value. Deterioration over a period of time. The opposite of *appreciation*. 2. In appraising, depreciation is the reduction in value of a property as measured from the cost to replace it. It is the difference between the replacement cost and the market value. 3. In accounting, it is a write-off (usually computed annually) of a portion of an asset on the records.

Deterioration The lowering of value of property.

Earnest money A purchaser's partial payment, as a show of good faith, to make a contract binding. A deposit; a down payment.

Earning-to-price ratio A ratio of the net income of property to the selling price.

Economic obsolescence A decline in the market value of property due to any external influence. An environmental decline that limits the highest and best use to which the property can be put.

Effective age A building's physical condition, not its actual age, determines its effective age. For appraisal purposes, it is an assumed age that would be equivalent to the physical condition of the structure; the better the condition, the lower the effective age.

Face value The apparent value. Value indicated on the outside. The value shown on the face of any instrument, such as stock certificates, bonds, bills, or currency.

Failure to perform Failure of one of the parties to a contract to perform what was agreed upon.

First lien The lien that takes legal priority over any other charges or encumbrances upon property. It is the one that must be completely satisfied before others are paid. A *first mortgage*.

First mortgage The mortgage on property that is superior to any other. The one that takes precedence over a junior or second mortgage. A *first lien*.

Foreclosure A legal action instituted by a mortgage holder, when a mortgage goes into default, to end all rights and possession of the mortgagor. The subject asset then becomes the property of the mortgagee.

Foreclosure sale A sale in which the property pledged as security for a debt is sold to pay the debt.

Forfeit To give up the right to or physical possession of something. Loss of anything of value because of failure to act or otherwise do what was agreed upon.

Free and clear A reference to ownership of property that is free of all indebtedness.

Functional obsolescence Defects in a structure that detract from its marketability and value.

Grace period A period when a mortgage payment or other debt becomes past due, and before it goes into default. Most mortgages provide for a specified period of time when it can be paid without penalty or default.

Gross income The total of money received from income property or a business, before operation expenses, taxes, depreciation, commissions, salaries, fees, and so forth are deducted.

Gross income multiplier A method of estimating the value of certain types of income properties by multiplying the gross income by an established multiplier. If, as an example, an apartment house is valued at 6X the gross income, and the gross income is $100,000, then the estimated value would be $600,000. Appraisal experts agree that this method, at best, should be used as a rule-of-thumb and only taken into account in conjunction with other appraisal techniques.

Income The financial benefits from business, labor, capital invested, or property. The monetary return or other advantageous benefits of an investment. The amount of gain received in money, goods, or services over a period of time.

Income approach to value A method of appraising property by basing the value upon the net amount of income produced by the property. It is calculated by subtracting the total income of the property from the expenses to determine the net profit. Also known as the *capitalization method*. (See *appraisal*.)

Income and expense statement A statement of income received from a property and an itemized list of expenses incurred in its operation.

Income property Property owned or purchased primarily for the monetary return it will bring. It may be classified as commercial, industrial, or residential.

Income tax Federal, state, and sometimes local taxes that are levied against the annual income of an individual or a corporation.

Incompetent A person who is not legally qualified to reach proper decisions.

Installment One of a series of payments of an obligation. Periodic, partial payments of a debt.

Installment sales contract A contract for the sale of property in which the buyer receives possession of the property, but not title to it, upon signing the contract. The buyer makes regular installment payments until the purchase price is reached. Only then does he receive the deed and title.

One reason for an installment contract being used, instead of a mortgage, is the ease and speed with which the property can be repossessed in the event of a default. This type of contract is also referred to as an *agreement for deed, contract for deed, conditional sales contract,* and a *land contract.*

Interest 1. A portion, share, or right in something. A partial but not complete ownership. Having an interest does not necessarily indicate possessing title, as for example, in a leasehold interest or mortgage. 2. The charge or rate paid for borrowing money; the compensation received for loaning it. (See *compound interest, simple interest.*)

Investment An amount of money, property, or other valuable asset expended for the purpose of making a profit at a later time.

Investor An individual who puts money into a business or real estate venture with the intention of realizing a satisfactory financial return on the capital invested.

Judgment 1. A considered opinion; a formal pronouncement; an estimate or evaluation. 2. A decree or finding handed down from a court of law following litigation. An order or pronouncement of a court.

Judgment lien A lien that binds the land of a debtor so that it proceeds can be used to satisfy a debt.

Judicial sale A sale of real or personal property ordered by a court or other authorized legal body.

Late charge A charge levied against installment loans and mortgage payments when not paid on time. It may take the form of a flat penalty fee or it can be a percentage of the periodic payment. The amount of the late charge is stated in the original instrument of indebtedness.

Lease A contract between the owner of property (lessor) and tenant (lessee) for the possession and use of the property for a stipulated period of time, in consideration for the payment of an agreed upon rent or for services rendered.

Lessee A tenant. The one to whom a lease is given to occupy premises for a given length of time and at a specified rate.

Lessor A landlord. The grantor of a lease. The one who leaves property to a tenant.

Leverage In real estate, the term means effective use of money. It is usually accomplished by investing the least amount of capital possible when acquiring property in order that it may bring the maximum percentage of return. This can be done by mortgaging to the highest amount that is practical. As long as the mortgage payments and operating expenses are not prohibitively high, the greatest yield on capital invested can generally be obtained.

Liability Any drawback, debt, or obligation. Something that acts as a disadvantage. An obligation or duty that must be performed. The opposite of *asset*.

Lien A charge or claim upon property that encumbers it until the obligation is satisfied. The property serves as the security.

Loan value The amount a lending institution will lend on the property.

Loan value ratio The ratio of the appraised value of property in proportion to the amount of the mortgage loan.

MAI Member Appraisal Institute.

Maintenance The painting, cleaning, and general repair work done to property and equipment to keep it productive and useful.

Marketable title Good title; clear title.

Market value The price that a property will bring under normal conditions on the open market. The amount that an owner, under no obligation or compulsion to sell, is willing to sell for, and the amount a buyer is freely willing to pay. The highest price an asset will bring under normal market conditions within a reasonable period of time.

Mechanic's lien A statutory lien levied on property by those who furnish material and labor for the construction of a building or other improvement. The lien attaches to the land as well as the structures upon it and establishes a priority of payment. In most states a mechanic's lien is created by statute.

Minor One who has not reached the age required to be legally recognized as an adult.

Misrepresentation A false presentation of the facts.

Mortgage A pledge of property as security for the payment of a debt.

Mortgagee The one who holds the mortgage as security for the money he has loaned on property. The lender or creditor.

Mortgagor The giver of a mortgage as security for money he borrows on his property.

Negative leverage When the cost to borrow money (interest) exceeds the return that money would bring, the resulting loss becomes leverage in reverse. (See *leverage*).

Neighborhood 1. A community of people living in a general vicinity. 2. The immediate proximity of property; the land that surrounds another parcel. A section; area.

Net income The money remaining after expenses are subtracted from the income. The profit.

Net worth   The current market value after totaling assets and subtracting liabilities.

Note   An instrument used as tangible proof that a person owes a certain sum of money to another and that he agrees to pay it under the specified terms and conditions. It is also called a *promissory note*.

Obsolescence   Passing out of style; outmoded; out of date.

Offer and acceptance   A willingness to buy under stated terms by the purchaser and an approval of those terms by the seller; a contract.

Operating income   Income received directly from property or from the operation of a business before expenses are deducted.

Operating ratio   The ratio of the expenses of running commercial property or a business to its gross income.

Opinion of title   An attorney's opinion as to how good the title to a specified piece of property is after studying the *abstract*.

Origination fee   In reference to mortgaging, it is a charge for establishing and processing a new mortgage loan.

Owner   The one possessing dominion or title to property. A person having a lawful interest in the land; the holder of the fee.

Paper   A jargon reference to the taking of a note or mortgage in lieu of cash.

Penalty   A loss sustained for not fulfilling an agreement.

PITI   An abbreviation for *principal, interest, taxes* and *insurance*.

Point   1. A "point" represents 1% of the principal amount. The term is most frequently used when referring to mortgage premiums. It is a method used by lenders to obtain additional revenues over the interest rate. 2. As used in legal descriptions, it is the extreme end of a boundary line.

Possession The act or state of possessing; the holding and peaceful enjoyment of property.

Prepayment clause A clause in a mortgage permitting the mortgagor to pay all or part of the unpaid balance before it becomes due, thereby saving the interest or clearing the way for a new mortgage.

Prepayment penalty A penalty imposed upon a mortgagor for paying the mortgage before it becomes due, when there is no *prepayment clause*.

Price The amount paid in legal tender, goods, or services; the consideration; purchase price.

Prime rate A term referring to the interest rate reserved by banks for prime or preferred borrowers.

Priority of lien The order in which a lien will be honored in relation to others.

Private property All land not held by a government. Individually owned property.

Property tax A tax levied on real and personal property.

Quitclaim deed The instrument used to remove any and all claims or interest in ownership that an individual may have without his warranting the quality or validity of the title.

Ratification Confirmation; affirmation.

Real estate The land itself and everything below, growing upon or attached to it. The physical substance of real property. Houses, trees, shrubs, fences, and what is permanently affixed to the land are classified as real estate. Anything else is personal property.

Real property Land itself, the improvements thereon, and the rights, title and interest one has in it. (See also *real estate*.)

Recourse Seeking aid in an effort to protect one's interest.

Redeem Repurchase; recover; reclaim, as when one liberates property from a lien by satisfactorily clearing that which encumbered it.

Redemption   The act of a party redeeming property he has put up as security for a loan by paying the indebtedness.

Refinance   To renew or extend existing financing or obtain another source.

Rent   The income received from leasing real estate.

Replacement cost   The amount of money that would be needed to replace the equivalent of a building, furnishings, or other asset.

Reproduction cost   The cost to duplicate an asset. (See *replacement cost.*)

Rescind   Call back; to make void; repeal; cancel, as when one rescinds a contract.

Sale   The change in ownership of property for a specified sum and under stipulated terms and conditions.

Salable   Property that can be readily sold.

Second loan; Second mortgage   A mortgage that is second in rank and subordinate to a first mortgage. Also called a *junior mortgage.*

Seller's market   When any commodity including real estate is in short supply, the seller is in a more commanding position.

Simple interest   Interest that is computed on the principal amount of a loan only. No amount need be paid for amassing interest, as occurs with a loan containing *compound interest.*

Solvent   The position of being able to pay one's financial and legal obligations; the ability to meet one's debts.

Special assessment   A special levy on property to pay for a specific public improvement to the property or in the immediate area, such as for road construction, sidewalks, sewers, street lights, and so forth.

Specific performance   Performing exactly, or as reasonably as possible, the terms of a contract. Fulfilling specifically as agreed.

Straight loan A loan in which only interest payments are periodically made with the entire principal amount becoming due at maturity.

Subordinated interest An interest or right in property that is inferior to another, such as a second mortgage being subordinate to a first.

Subordination When a lien holder agrees to place his interest in lesser rank than another's. This frequently occurs when the seller of vacant land, in order to make the sale, takes back a mortgage and agrees to lower its rank to second position behind a construction or permanent loan.

Subordination clause The clause in an instrument which states that a lien or mortgage shall be inferior to that of another.

Title As applied to real estate, title indicates lawful ownership and right to property. It is the fee position. Title to property is that *bundle of rights* an owner possesses.

Title insurance 1. Insuring the title to property. An insurance policy issued to the landowner indemnifying him up to a specified amount against having a defective or unmarketable title as long as he owns the property. 2. Title policies are also issued to the mortgagee as protection against loss in the event title to the mortgaged property proves defective. These are referred to as mortgage policies or loan policies.

Title report A report of the condition of the title to a specific piece of property after an examination of the abstract has been made.

Title search An examination of the public records tracing the chain of title to a specific property to the present owner, and determining if it is clear and marketable or is in any way defective.

Trust A position of responsibility given to one to act in the best interests of another. A trust can be either expressed or implied. It is a right that is enforceable in a court of equity.

Trustee 1. A party who legally holds property in trust for others. 2. One placed in a position of responsibility.

Trustor The originator or creator of a trust.

Unrecorded instrument Any document that has not been publicly recorded.

Usable income Cash flow. Spendable income.

Useful life A property's life as long as it proves of utility to the owner.

Vacancy factor The percentage of a building's unrented space during a given period. It is sometimes figured as the gross income that a building loses due to vacancies. In estimating rental income, the vacancy factor is deducted from the gross rental when at capacity.

Valuation A term synonymous with appraising.

Value The worth of one thing in comparison with another. The market value.

Void Nullify; of no legal significance, force, or effect. Not binding.

Warranty deed A deed in which the grantor guarantees that he is giving the grantee and his heirs good title free of encumbrances. It is recognized as the highest form of deed, as the grantor agrees to defend the title and possession against all claims.

White elephant Property difficult to dispose of.

Wrap-around mortgage A refinancing technique in which the lender assumes payment of the existing mortgage and gives a new, increased mortgage to the borrower at a higher interest rate. As defined by its name, the new mortgage "wraps around" the original one.

Yield What an investment or property will return.

Suggested reading

Allen, Robert G. *Nothing Down*. New York: Simon & Schuster, 1980.

Barrett, G. Vincent, and Blair, John P. *Foundations of Real Estate Analysis*. New York: Macmillan Publishing Co., Inc., 1981.

French, William B., and Lusk, Harold F. *Law of the Real Estate Business* (4th ed.). Homewood, Ill.: Richard D. Irwin, Inc., 1979.

Jorgensen, Erick. *Successful Real Estate Sales & Agreements*. San Francisco: Canfield Press, 1976.

Kratovil, Robert, and Werner, Raymond J. *Modern Mortgage Law & Practice* (2nd ed.). Englewood Cliffs, N.J.: Prentice-Hall, Inc., 1981.

Nesson, Robert L. *The Real Estate Book*. Boston: Little, Brown, & Co., 1981.

Pace, Peter. *Complete Handbook of Real Estate Math*. Reston, Va.: Reston Publishing Co., 1982.

Seldin, Maury, and Swesink, Richard H. *Real Estate Investment Strategy*. New York: John Wiley & Sons Inc., 1979.

Temple, Douglas M. *Real Estate Investment for the 80's*. Chicago: Contemporary Books, 1981.

Van Horne, James C. *Real Estate Principles & Practices*. Englewood Cliffs, N.J.: Prentice-Hall, 1981.

Index

American Land Title Association (ALTA), 169
Abstract, 168
Acceleration clauses, 92
Address, 128
Annual gross income, 99
Appraisal, 124
Appreciation, 2, 100, 101, 104
Assets, 117

Balloon payment, 6, 17, 18, 46, 138
Bankruptcies, 121
Bigger fool theory, 100, 105
Bind, 108
Breach of contract, 108
Building components, 102
Business relationship, 173, 175

Buyer credit form, 116

CAP rate, 98, 99, 100
Calculators, 141
Capital gains, 151, 156
Capital gains tax, 156
Capitalization rate, 98, 99
Cash flow, 4, 13
Chains—see *contract chains*
Commercial lender, 114
Comparison of price vs. value, 103
Complete income analysis, 101
Computations, 141
Computing values of property, 103
Condition, 130
Condominium, 129
Contract chain, 36–44, 94, 112

Contract sale, 26
Conventional financing, 11, 13
Conventional mortgages, 26, 94
Cosigner, 122
Cosmetic blemishes, 8
Creative financing, 16, 22, 105
Credit, 15
Credit bureau, 120, 121
Credit check, 43, 115, 118, 120
Credit evaluation, 122
Credit form, 115, 116
Credit life insurance, 123
Credibility, 17
Creditor, 119

Damages, 108, 111
Deed, trust, 113
Deed, quitclaim, 113
Default, 20, 167
Deficiency judgments, 122
Delapidated property, 90
Delinquent, 111
Deposits, 76
Design, 8, 127, 130
Discount, 112
Discount for cash, 104
Discount rate, 150
Discounted interest rate, 152
Discounted price, 150
Documentation of the loan, 124
Do-it-yourself, 89
Double closings, 86
Down payment, 60
Due on sale clause, 92–95

Earnest money, 28, 32
Earnest-money contract, 30, 31
Economy, 14
Emotional attachment, 18, 174
Escrow, 113
Escrow agent, 113
Estimated value, 99, 100, 103, 151
Exposure, 128
Exterior design, 127, 130

Fair market value, 97
Federal income tax, 156
Final agreement, 33
Forced appreciation, 3
Forecloses, 93, 106, 108, 109, 111
Forfeiture, 106, 107, 108, 110
Free and clear, 36

Garnishment of wages, 122
Goals, 2
Grace period, 167
Gross income, 99
Gross monthly income, 122
Gross rent multipliers, 100

Handyman special, 88–91, 131
High-yielding real estate investments, 153

Income, 116
Income approach, 99
Income producing asset, 119
Income statement, 7, 64
Income taxes, 4, 155
Inexperience, 12
Inspection, 165
Installment contract, 14
Installment sales contract, 36
Institutional financing, 24, 26
Insurance, 164, 165
Interest income, 151, 157
Interest rate, 60, 104
Interest table, 142–147
Interior decorator, 131
Interior design, 127, 130
Investment capital, 151
Investments in contracts, 151

Land sales contract, 36
Legal age, 122
Liabilities, 118
Liability, 19
Lifetime exclusion, 157
Liquidated damages, 108

Loan-payoff period, 60
Location, 6, 127, 128

Market approach, 102
Market method, 98, 102
Market value, 97, 102
Marketable title, 97
Merchandise for downpayment, 79
Mortgage insurance, 124

Negative cash flow, 19, 56, 69
Neighborhood, 127, 128
Net Operating Income (NOI), 99
No down payment, 69
No money down, 68

Objective attitude, 174
Offer to purchase, 28, 30, 31
Operating expeditures, 60, 61, 66
Ordinary income, 156
Over-priced, 69
Owner financing, 24, 36
Owner-financing contracts, 94

Paint-by-the-number, 28
Payment structures, 166
Penalties, 167
Present value, 134
Price, 96, 104
Price ratio to income, 99
Price vs. value, 69, 96, 103, 104
Positive cash flow, 101
Professionally serviced contracts, 124
Property appreciation, 104
Property, condition of, 8
Property, inspections, 165
Property taxes, 155, 163, 164

Qualifications, 91
Qualifying the buyer, 116
Quantity survey, 102
Quitclaim deed (see *Deed, quitclaim*)

Ran-out-of-money sale, 90
Ratio, price-to-income, 122
Receiver, 111
Red flags, 121
Redemption, 109, 112
Redemption period, 109, 112
Refinance, 17
Remaining unpaid balance, 49
Renegotiation, 112
Rent, 61
Replacement cost, 98
Replacement cost method, 102
Replacement value, 102
Repossess, 94
Researching titles, 94
Resources, 6, 7
Risk, 7, 8

Sales price, 97
Screen, 175
Second closing, 84
Second mortgage, 27
Securities, 117
Seller's income statement, 63
Serviced contracts, 124
Shop properties, 175
Simple income approach, 100
Speculate, 14
Speculation, 18
Standard forms, 28
State income tax, 156
Structural damage, 8, 127
Subordinations, 82

Tax shelters, 4
Taxes, income, 4, 155, 156
Taxes, property, 155, 162
Taxing authority, 155
Terms, 4
Three-party agreement, 29
Time under contract, 32
Time value of money, 134
Title insurance, 168
Title search, 152

True market value, 98
Trust deed, 113
Trustor, 113
Two-party agreement, 29

Underlying debts, 111
Uniform documentation, 124
Uniform sales contract, 107

Unpaid balance, 48
Unqualified buyer, 114

Vacancy factor, 65
Value, 96, 104

Waiver, 95
Wraparound contract, 27